30-Minute Meals

Created and designed by the editorial staff of Ortho Books

Project Editor	Anne Coolman
Writer	Susan E. Mitchell
Designer	James Stockton
Photographers	David Fischer and
	Patrick Lyons
Food Stylist	Bunny Martin
Photographic Stylist	Carol Hacker
Associate Editor	Beverley DeWitt

Ortho Books

Publisher
Robert L. Iacopi

Editorial Director
Min S. Yee

Managing Editor
Anne Coolman

Horticultural Editor
Michael D. Smith

Senior Editor
Kenneth R. Burke

Production Manager
Laurie S. Blackman

Horticulturist
Michael D. McKinley

Editors
Barbara J. Ferguson
Susan M. Lammers
Sally W. Smith

Production Assistants
Darcie S. Furlan
Julia W. Hall

National Sales Manager
Garry P. Wellman

Operations/Distribution
William T. Pletcher

Operations Assistant
Donna M. White

Administrative Assistant
Georgiann Wright

Address all inquiries to:
Ortho Books
Chevron Chemical Company
Consumer Products Division
575 Market Street
San Francisco, CA 94105

First Printing in August, 1982

1 2 3 4 5 6 7 8 9
82 83 84 85 86 87

ISBN 0-89721-006-9

Library of Congress Catalog Card
Number 82-82158

Chevron Chemical Company
575 Market Street, San Francisco, CA 94105

Acknowledgments
Food and Wine Consultants
and Testers:
James R. Bartlett
Annette C. Fabri
Connie Krough-Wirt
Lorinda Moholt
Carolyn E. Petersen
Maureen Reynolds

Assistant Designer:
Karen Tucker

Assistant Food Stylist:
Karen Ray Gibson

Copyediting:
Editcetera
Berkeley, CA

Typography:
CBM Type
Sunnyvale, CA

Color Separations:
Color Tech
Redwood City, CA

Special Thanks to:
Mary Concelmo
Lyn Fenner
Joyce Wilder-Jones

Cover Photograph
Kiwi fruit makes a delicious,
unusual addition to the classic
Meunière (lemon-butter-parsley)
sauce, and shredded squash in
two colors cooks even more
quickly than the 10-minute
entrée. With color, texture, and a
wonderful blend of flavors, this
Seafood with Kiwi menu typifies
what you can do in 30 minutes.
(See page 17 for recipes.)

Back Cover
Upper left: Broiled Salmon
Steaks with Tomatoes au Gratin
(Menu 7, page 21).

Upper right: Skillet Vegetarian
Delight (Menu 43, page 63).

Lower left: Breakfast Omelet
technique (Filling Variations,
page 85).

Lower right: Korean Chicken
Thighs with Wild-and-White Rice
(Menu 16, page 31).

Title page
Writer Susan Mitchell, a Cordon
Bleu chef and culinary expert,
demonstrates the fun and flair
of 30-minute cooking. For a
discussion of her techniques,
see pages 5–11.

30-Minute Meals

Quick-Cooking Basics 5

50 Easy Dinner Menus 13

Quick Breakfasts & Lunches 79

Quick-Cooking Basics

Your time may be short, but your meals can still be fresh and delicious. Learn quick-cooking techniques, which utensils work best, and what foods to keep on hand. All help you spend less time cooking and more time enjoying your meals.

What is a 30-minute meal? Simple, fresh foods prepared with tried-and-true quick-cooking techniques. And what are these techniques? (1) Organizing your kitchen for efficiency; (2) gathering all your utensils and ingredients before you do anything else; (3) chopping, slicing, and measuring all your ingredients before you actually begin to cook; (4) preparing several dishes at once using quick-cooking methods; and (5) serving and garnishing the meal in ways that add to its appeal.

The technique that makes the biggest difference and takes the most practice is cooking several dishes at once. If you're preparing a complete top-of-the-stove meal, you may have something going on all 4 burners. The first time you attempt this, it's easy to feel as if the whole process might get away from you at any minute. But it won't, and as you cook more meals in this fashion, your skill will increase rapidly. This approach to cooking is not only fun and satisfying, but your family and friends will also be impressed with your culinary talents.

Gradually you'll be able to add even more flair to your cooking: keeping the kitchen neat and tidy while you whip up an incredible meal; carrying on a conversation without missing a beat; experimenting with garnishes, or directing a kitchen assistant or two and being ready to eat in no time at all.

The idea of the 30-minute timetable is *not* to become frazzled trying to "beat the clock," particularly at first. One tester's first effort took 45 minutes, but as she became used to the techniques, her

preparation times fell well within the 30-minute range. The best approach is to prepare the menus without constantly watching the clock — then if it takes you more than 30 minutes, look for ways to cut down your time. You may discover, as another tester did, that having all the utensils out and ready really *does* make a difference — it took him more than 3 minutes just to locate the whisk when he needed it. You'll also find that some menus can easily be prepared in less than 30 minutes — and that you'll need all the time for others.

No cookbook is a panacea for everything, and there will be nights when your idea of a quick meal is putting a roast and potatoes in the oven and lying down for an hour; or having someone else cook; or going to a restaurant; or skipping dinner entirely. What *30-Minute Meals* will do, however, is help you discover the types of foods and cooking techniques that make fast, delicious, attractive meals possible. Use this book to have some fun, to develop your own shortcuts, and to spend less time cooking and more time enjoying great meals.

The Plan of the Book

The balance of this chapter describes the basics of the quick-cooking approach. The second chapter — 50 Easy Dinner Menus — makes up the heart of the book. It's not essential to follow each menu to the letter, but the cooking plan with each one outlines the approach to take until the process becomes second nature. A special section on simple but elegant desserts follows the dinner menus. The last chapter — Quick Breakfasts & Lunches — consists of alternatives to routine or grab-on-the-run fare, to revitalize your interest in these sometimes neglected meals.

Cooking quickly gives you more time to serve food with style. With only one set of dishes but a variety of tablecloths, placemats, and napkins, you can vary the appearance of every meal.

Kitchen Basics

Whether prepared in a leisurely fashion or in a rush, a good meal requires organization on the part of the cook. One way to reduce the time it takes to put a meal on the table is by fixing a casserole or a stew ahead of time and heating it just before serving. Another way is to concentrate your cooking efforts and prepare a meal from scratch in just 30 minutes. In the first approach, planning and advance preparation let you limit the time you must spend in the kitchen immediately before the meal. In the second approach, planning and efficiency allow you to limit the time you must spend in the kitchen until just before mealtime. This type of organization — in kitchen layout and storage, menu planning and shopping, staples, and cooking equipment — reduces the time it takes to prepare any meal.

Layout and Storage. Obviously, you don't have to remodel your kitchen to cook 30-minute meals, but you can improve an awkward kitchen floor plan with something as common as a movable chopping-block cart. It reduces the number of steps you have to take and increases your usable counter space. Also take a few minutes to inventory the items you use most frequently — utensils, chopping blocks, spices, lids, oven mitts, and so on. Then stand at your stove and figure out the best storage arrangement for easy access to all of them. Do the same for your countertop preparation area. Make

the necessary changes, and take advantage of drawer dividers; containers for storing utensils by the stove; and wall, door, and ceiling racks. Having what you need close at hand saves much more time than you may realize and will reduce mealtime aggravation.

Menu Planning and Shopping. The idea of menu planning is not to eliminate flexibility or spontaneity but to ensure that you have the ingredients you need. By getting into the habit, you'll cut grocery bills, save time, and most important, give yourself options. Many of the pasta or rice-based main dishes and the soup-and-sandwich meals can be made from staples; they are perfect for nights when you don't feel like cooking what you had planned. For speed in shopping, type up a basic list ordered to reflect the layout of your supermarket and the route you generally take through it. Make photocopies of the list and then check off items as you run short. Post both menus and shopping list in a convenient place and check each morning for foods that need defrosting.

Staples. A well-stocked pantry and freezer are an important part of the 30-minute philosophy — and staples mean more than just salt, flour, sugar, and milk. To prepare these menus, you'll need to have the items in the chart below on hand. Add other family favorites to your list of pantry essentials.

Staples for 30-Minute Meals

To simplify your shopping list, cut down on trips to the grocery store, and allow for flexibility at mealtime, make the foods on this chart part of the supplies you keep on hand for quick breakfasts, lunches, and dinners. The chart also includes tips for storage of those staples that can be chopped, minced, or cooked in quantity ahead of time to speed meal preparation.

Poultry, Fish, and Meat. Frozen in meal-size quantities, **precooked chicken** makes a speedy dinner entrée or salad. (Stewing a whole chicken or two is simple, economical, and takes little attention.) Freeze the stock in an ice tray (for individual cubes) or in larger containers. Keep canned **chicken and beef broth** and bottled **clam juice** in your pantry to use full strength in soups, as a base for sauces, or to add flavor to rice or pilafs. **Canned or frozen seafood** — shrimp, crabmeat, salmon, tuna — are handy additions to omelets, pasta, soups, and salads. Keep **patés** and **cold cuts** on hand for sandwiches, hors d'oeuvres, omelets, and salads.

Vegetables. In all but the summer months, **canned tomatoes** (whole and stewed) are generally more flavorful than fresh. **Frozen peas** (in bags rather than boxes) are a quick way to add interest to pasta, entrées,

and salads. Also keep canned **tomato or vegetable juice cocktail** available to flavor sauces. Mincing **onion** in quantity saves time: freeze it in recipe-size amounts (¼ cupfuls). The same is true of **garlic**: mince; cover with oil; and store, tightly capped, in the refrigerator for up to a month.

Fruits. You'll need **fresh citrus fruits** for juice (or **bottled lemon and lime juice**) and for garnish. Especially during the winter months, stock **dried, canned, and frozen fruits** for quick desserts and breakfasts, and to add to dinner entrées. A selection of **frozen and bottled fruit juices** is also useful.

Dairy Products. For dinner sauces, soups, and desserts, stock **heavy cream** (or its low-calorie substitute, **evaporated skim milk**) yogurt, sour cream, nonfat dry milk, and **ice cream** or **sherbet. Cheeses** — Monterey jack, Cheddar, Parmesan or Romano, and low-calorie ricotta — are used in many

of the recipes. Grate hard cheese in quantity and store in a container in the freezer; it will not freeze solid. **Hard-cooked eggs** are musts for salads, sandwich fillings, and garnishes.

Pasta/Breads/Cereals/Baked Goods. Dried pasta — in assorted sizes, shapes, and colors — can always be turned into a quick meal. The same is true of **white rice. Bread crumbs** make crunchy toppings and give texture to coatings. **Frozen tortillas, crepes,** and **croissants** let you create quick entrées or out-of-the-ordinary breakfasts and lunches. Use **cereals** in cookies and parfaits, as well as for breakfast. **Cookies** and **poundcake** provide quick dessert possibilities.

Herbs, Spices, and Condiments. A well-stocked spice shelf cuts down trips to the grocery. And fresh herbs, which have more flavor than dried, can be stored in water in the refrigerator or frozen

when in season. **Parsley, watercress, cilantro, basil, oregano,** and **rosemary** are some of the common ones. Sprigs of fresh herbs also make attractive garnishes. Well-wrapped **ginger root** can be frozen indefinitely.

Vegetable and olive oil; vinegars (red and white wine, cider, and herb); **Worcestershire, hot pepper,** and **soy sauce; Dijon-style mustard;** and **Mexican salsa** flavor many entrées. **Syrups** — maple, berry, and chocolate — spark up breakfasts and desserts. And **bittersweet chocolate, nuts, raisins,** and **grated coconut** should be kept on hand.

Wines and Liqueurs. Sherry, Madeira, Marsala, Cognac, and **brandy** — or the **red or white wine** you will drink with dinner — flavor some of the entrées. Liqueurs such as **Grand Marnier, Cointreau, Amaretto,** and **Frangelica** add their distinct tastes to desserts — and create drama when flamed.

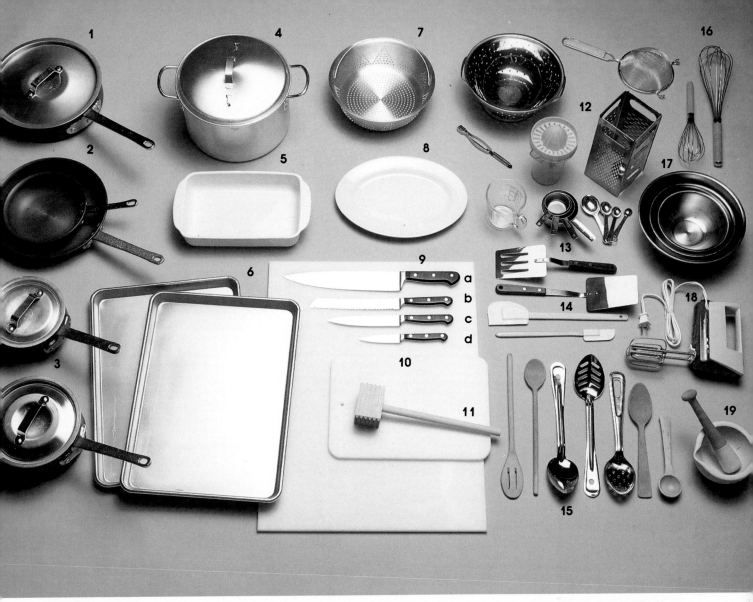

With the basic equipment shown in this photograph, you can prepare any of the 30-minute meals. Each piece is identified in the text below.

Equipment. You don't need a pressure cooker, a microwave or convection oven, a slow cooker, or for most of the recipes, a blender or food processor to prepare 30-minute meals. But if you do have this equipment, use it when it will save you time. Information on adapting standard techniques to microwave cooking can be found on page 10.

To prepare the menus in this book, you'll need the following (identified by number in the photograph above): **(1)** Large skillets with lids — two 8- or 10-inch for butter-steaming or sautéing vegetables. **(2)** Large and small sauté pans — 12-inch, heavy-bottomed, with slanted sides; 6-inch for toasting nuts or seeds and heating alcohol. **(3)** Small and medium saucepans with lids — 1- or 1½-quart for preparing sauces, melting butter, and heating alcohol; 2½- or 3-quart for cooking rice and vegetables. **(4)** Large pot with lid — 6-quart or more for cooking pasta, stewing chickens, and preparing soup. **(5)** Shallow baking dish — 1½- or 2-quart for casseroles. **(6)** Heavy baking sheets — two, for toasting bread and preparing pancakes, French toast, and potatoes. **(7)** Steamer — perforated insert that fits the large pot or medium saucepan. **(8)** Ovenproof serving platter — for keeping meat or fish warm while preparing sauces (a shallow casserole can be substituted). **(9)** Knives — one of each: **(a)** 10- to 12-inch chopping, made of heavy steel;

(b) serrated bread knife; **(c)** 6½- to 8-inch utility, made of stainless steel with thin, slender blade; **(d)** 3- or 4-inch paring. **(10)** Polyethylene or wood chopping boards — small, for garlic and onions; large, for everything else. **(11)** Mallet — for pounding cutlets. **(12)** Colander — for draining pasta and vegetables; Medium strainer — for rinsing rice or thawing frozen fruits and vegetables; Vegetable peeler; Lemon/lime juicer — for straining seeds automatically; and Four-sided, stainless-steel grater — for grating vegetables, hard cheeses, and nuts. **(13)** Measuring cups and spoons — liquid and dry. **(14)** Spatulas — metal and rubber. **(15)** Long-handled spoons — regular and slotted. **(16)** Large and small balloon whisks — for beating sauces. **(17)** Stainless-steel mixing bowls — in assorted sizes. **(18)** Electric hand mixer — for beating egg whites. **(19)** Mortar and pestle — good for crushing garlic and spices.

Optional but useful: Tongs; Long-handled fork; Hard-cooked egg slicer; Tomato wedger; Butter molds; Mushroom brush; Dredger (metal container with perforated top, for shaking flour, sugar, cinnamon onto foods); Small grater for ginger root and nutmeg; Serrated fruit knife with curved end; Apple corer; Poultry shears for cutting whole chickens into pieces; Individual casserole dishes; Blender, food processor, and toaster oven.

Preparing to Cook

What you do before you turn on the stove is at least as important as your proficiency in cooking. First, read the recipes and the cooking plan for the menu to familiarize yourself with the instructions and the overall process. Then gather everything you will need — ingredients, equipment and utensils, cutting board, and serving platters. It's tempting to ignore this step (after all, it will only take a second to get out the measuring cup), but don't be fooled. Finding things while you're cooking takes more time than you think.

Preparation also includes measuring, chopping, and mincing. This is what enables you to cook a number of dishes at one time. Keep the following preparation tips in mind:

■ Invest in high-quality knives, keep them sharp, and store them properly.

■ Use a cutting board large enough to accommodate your ingredients. The polyethylene ones now available are lightweight, can be scrubbed with soap and water with no ill effects, and can even be washed in the dishwasher.

■ To cut up anything, begin by producing a flat surface; then turn the item flat-side down for safe, efficient slicing.

■ For mincing or chopping, use the professional chef's technique: keeping the point of the knife stationary, lift the handle up and down and pivot it from side to side.

■ If more than one item will be added to a dish at the same time and all must be minced, do them all at once.

■ When slicing or trimming vegetables such as carrots, celery, or beans, do 3 or 4 stalks or pieces at a time.

Quick-Cooking Methods

As noted on page 5, the quick-cooking approach includes the ability to juggle a number of dishes all at once. This is where familiarity with the recipes and cooking plan pays off — in facility at moving from one dish to another, checking, adding, and stirring. The main thing to keep in mind is that *you* are directing the action. If something seems to be cooking too fast, reduce the heat. If it takes you longer to complete a step than you thought it would, slow down other dishes that are already underway. Gradually, the timing will become part of your mental repertoire and you won't have to keep referring to the cooking plan. And remember, if you're not used to cooking this way, trying to do so while keeping dinner guests entertained is not the best way to start. Either put them to work, or try your first 30-minute meal when you can concentrate on what you're doing.

Most of the recipes in this book call for thin meat or poultry cutlets, fish fillets or small whole fish, ground meats, and chops. And most are cooked by one of these methods: sauté or stir-fry, broil, poach, and steam. Some recipes also use a quick bake — foods are heated and partly cooked on top of the stove and then placed in a hot oven to finish cooking or to brown. If you are unfamiliar with any of these quick-cooking methods, the explanations in any number of basic cookbooks will help.

Sauté. The sauté method — cooking thin, tender pieces of meat, fish, and vegetables in a little oil and butter over high heat — seals in both flavor and juices. For perfect sautéed foods that are not greasy, keep these points in mind:

Getting out all the menu ingredients and doing your chopping, slicing, and mincing before you begin to cook is an important, basic quick-cooking technique. Here, the ingredients needed for Chicken à la Reimann (page 29) are assembled for efficient preparation.

■ Use a mixture of butter and oil; oil helps butter withstand high temperatures without burning. (If cholesterol is a concern, omit the butter and use low or no-cholesterol oil. The flavor of the food will be a bit different, but the sauce will generally mask this.)

■ The butter and oil must be hot (but not smoking) when the food is added to the pan. This quick sear forms the golden-brown surface characteristic of sautéed foods.

■ Overcooking will toughen meats and poultry and cause fish and many vegetables to fall apart. If you are using frozen fish, be sure it is completely thawed (and drained and patted dry) before you sauté it. Otherwise, it will be watery and may not be completely cooked in the center. Poaching is a better alternative for partially thawed fish.

■ For foods ¼-inch thick, sauté times are generally no more than 5 minutes per side.

■ For calves' liver, boned chicken or turkey breast slices, and thin fish fillets, a cooking time as short as 3 minutes per side can be sufficient.

■ When the edges of a piece of food begin to curl, the piece is usually ready to be turned.

■ Cooking times are given in all the recipes, but develop your judgment as to when foods are cooked to your liking.

Broil. Broiling — cooking under high heat without added fat — is also speedy and best for thicker meat or fish.

■ For a browned exterior without overcooking the interior, the broiler must be hot (at 550°F) when foods are put under it. The cooking plans remind you to preheat the broiler in time for it to reach the proper temperature.

■ To keep dry-fleshed fish or meats with little fat from drying out, brush with melted butter or oil before broiling.

■ Generally, broil 1-inch-thick meat a minimum of 4 inches from the heat source. The thicker the piece, the further from the heat it should be placed — and the longer it will take to cook.

Poach. Poaching — gently simmering fish, seafood, poultry, or vegetables in seasoned liquid — is a low-calorie way of preparing food. For best results, the poaching liquid (water, wine, fish or chicken stock) should be hot when the food is added to it. Then reduce the heat and cook until the food is just tender.

Steam. Vegetables retain more nutrients and flavor and require little attention when steamed. The recipes in this book use two methods — steaming over rapidly boiling water and steaming in butter and water.

■ To steam vegetables over boiling water, use a metal steamer designed for the purpose or substitute a colander. Place the steaming rack over a few inches of water in a 2- or 3-quart saucepan with a tight-fitting lid. When the water boils, add the vegetables. Depending on their size, steaming will take from 5 to 20 minutes.

■ Butter-steaming — cooking vegetables in a little butter and water in a tightly covered skillet — is an excellent method for long, thin vegetables such as asparagus or whole green beans. It's also a very quick way to cook cut-up vegetables, because the skillet offers a large surface area over which to spread them. And, butter-steaming flavors vegetables as they cook. The cooking times in this book produce tender-crisp vegetables.

Cooking four items at once is easy when the ingredients are chopped and ready. Chicken à la Reimann (shown in its preparation stages on the facing page) nears completion: the broccoli sauté (top left), almonds (top right), rice pilaf (bottom right), and the entrée (bottom left).

Serving and Garnishing Foods

Quick cooking is both fun in itself and the means to an end — enjoying relaxed, tasty, *attractive* meals. China, silver, and candles aren't the only ways to dress up a table. And you don't need three or four sets of dishes to have variety at mealtime. Use inexpensive items like placemats, napkins, and a few coordinated tablecloths to create different moods. Find small ways to make your table look special every night — and to change its appearance from week to week. Switch from a tablecloth to placemats or vice versa. Even a change of napkins makes a difference. Use small blooming plants — primroses, violets, crocus — or fragrant herbs as individual decorations; place the pots in colorful woven baskets or cover them with napkins. Changing wine or water glasses or adding a set of flatware with colorful plastic handles are simple, inexpensive ways to give your table a new look. Unusual serving bowls, platters, and pitchers do the same. The photographs throughout this book should give you many new ideas — you'll see how the same dishes can be coordinated with a variety of table coverings to make them seem new and different.

The way in which the food itself is presented — arrangement, color, and texture — really does affect its taste. If served with style, even the simplest food seems more flavorful. Good restaurants know this, and use it to their advantage — especially in garnishing foods for eye appeal. Garnishes can be complicated or simple, but they all whet the appetite and provide color contrast and textural interest. Cut in a variety of shapes, many vegetables and fruits are pretty as well as edible additions to any plate, and nuts, cheese, and other dairy products add both texture and flavor as toppings.

The garnishes and toppings listed below are easy to make and they add appeal to any menu. Each is identified by number in the photograph on the opposite page. Beginning at top left (and moving clockwise or from left to right within groupings), they are: (1) Nuts — whole toasted almonds, pecans, slivered and sliced almonds, and walnuts. (2) Fresh fruits — (a) pineapple, orange, and lemon wedges; (b) citrus twists and kiwi rounds; (c) nectarine and peach slices; (d) orange segments; (e) avocado and cantaloupe balls; (f) cherry, strawberry, and grapes; and (g) grated lemon, lime, and orange peel (zest). (3) Preserved and dried fruits — watermelon pickle in a lettuce leaf, dates, and golden raisins. (4) Fresh herbs — sprigs of oregano, rosemary, watercress, and parsley. (5) Cheese — shredded Cheddar and grated Parmesan. (6) Dairy products — sour cream topped with a sprig of rosemary. (7) Croutons — plain and flavored. (8) Flavored butters — orange and herb. (9) Hard-cooked egg — sieved yolk and slices. (10) Vegetables — (a) scallions — whole, fans, and chopped; (b) mushrooms — fluted caps and slices; (c) cherry tomatoes — whole and halves; tomato wedges on a lettuce leaf; (d) carrots — curls, sticks, and rounds; (e) cucumbers — slices and twists; and (f) radishes — roses, whole, and slices. (11) Flower petals or blossoms (unsprayed) — violets and nasturtiums. (12) Coconut — shredded. (13) Chocolate — curls and grated. (14) Mint.

The Microwave and 30-Minute Meals

Although a microwave oven cannot sauté or broil meats, it can be used for other cooking tasks in these 30-minute meals and has certain advantages. It provides another place to cook, can speed cleanup time by allowing you to cook and serve in the same dish, and will keep the kitchen cool when used to heat bread or rolls. It also conserves nutrients, particularly water-soluble vitamins, and saves electric energy. Try using yours for some of the cooking tasks listed below.

■ To cook **chicken breasts** for use in salads, soups, or fillings for entrées, microwave 1 halved breast in a covered casserole with ¼ cup vermouth or chicken broth and ¼ cup green onion for 8 to 10 minutes. Cool and cut up.

■ For the calorie-conscious, 1 pound of **fish** steams moist and tender in its own juices in 5 to 6 minutes. It tastes as if it were poached.

■ Fresh **vegetables**, cut as directed in these recipes, take almost as long to cook in a microwave (including standing time) as when they are sautéed or steamed on top of the stove. But, using the microwave frees the stove, and the vegetables will need little attention. If the recipe calls for steaming a vegetable before puréeing it or before a final sauté, try doing this in the microwave to save a few minutes.

A pound of most vegetables, cut in even-size pieces, will cook in 7 minutes. Root vegetables take 2 to 3 minutes more; very tender vegetables such as snow peas, 2 to 3 minutes less. Add little or no water and cook vegetables covered. Shake or stir once during cooking. Allow to stand 3 minutes after removing from microwave, to finish cooking internally.

■ Warm a **lemon or lime** for 30 seconds before squeezing; you will get more juice.

■ To toast ½ cup **almonds**, melt 1 tablespoon butter, add almonds, and microwave 2 minutes, stirring occasionally.

■ Heat **brandy** or other liqueurs for flamed entrées and desserts for 15 to 30 seconds. Pour over dish and ignite.

■ To warm **syrups** for waffles or pancakes, heat in a pitcher for 1 to 1½ minutes.

■ Heat **bread and rolls** in a serving basket until warm to the touch; they will be hot inside.

■ Use the microwave to simplify preparation of **staples**: it can dry bread cubes for **crumbs or croutons** (4 cups cubes, ⅓ cup melted butter, and choice of seasonings; cook on full power for 8 to 10 minutes, stirring occasionally) and can dry fresh **herbs** (microwave ½ cup leaves between paper towels 2 minutes).

■ A bonus: With a microwave, the 30-minute cook can add **baked potatoes** to meals. Cook 4 to 5 minutes and then let rest, wrapped in a towel or aluminum foil, another 5 minutes to finish cooking. Flesh will be fluffy and moist but skin will not be crisp.

Right: Attractive garnishes and tasty toppings take only minutes to make, but add dash to everyday meals and simple foods. Each of the items shown in the photograph on the facing page is identified in the text above.

50
Easy Dinner Menus

Spice up your evening meals with these quick, delicious entrées and vegetable dishes, and top them off with simple but special desserts. Whether you're cooking for family or guests, these menus look and taste like they took hours to prepare.

The 50 dinner menus in this chapter are designed for the quick-cooking enthusiast — the recipes are simple, and preparation is both efficient and enjoyable. On those nights when you want to take a more leisurely approach to cooking, you can simply allow more time and slow down the process. Either way, the result will be a delicious meal everyone can enjoy.

Select a week's menus at one time or choose whatever sounds good to you day by day. For easy selection, the menus are arranged by the type of entrée — fish, poultry, veal, beef, liver, pork, lamb, pasta, skillet casserole, salad, soup, and sandwich. Dessert ideas and recipes follow the dinner menus.

All the recipes serve 4 adults. If you are cooking for 2 or 6 or for small children, increase or reduce the ingredients to suit the appetites of your diners. If you're cooking for more than 4, however, preparing those menus that involve lots of chopping, mincing, or sautéing will probably take more than 30 minutes.

The 50 menus run the gamut from simple family fare to more elegant (and sometimes more expensive) meals that you might serve to company. A few of the menus are designed especially for summertime dining or as light suppers; others are more appropriate for colder weather. But most can be served at any time of the year simply by substituting what is in season for what is unavailable.

The side dishes selected to accompany each entrée are suggestions for combining complementary foods, not absolute musts. Keeping in

mind color, texture, and flavor, substitute other vegetables or starches to suit your preference, and look through the book for new recipes using your favorites. Of course, following the suggested menu can be a good way to introduce yourself and your family to unfamiliar foods and to new ways of preparing old favorites.

Don't overlook the variations that accompany many of the menus. They increase entrée possibilities substantially. In fact, from the 50 menus that follow, you can prepare at least 115 different entrées. And you can also use sauces for one type of meat on another — increasing the number of different entrées even more. Use your imagination and follow your preferences to expand dinner possibilities even further. And, use the quick-cooking techniques explained in Chapter 1 and the ideas in these menus to adapt favorite recipes for speedier preparation.

Do use the cooking plans to guide you in your first attempts at quick cooking. The philosophy behind them is simple — begin with the dish that takes the longest to cook *and* that can wait the longest before serving. This generally means the starch (rice or potatoes) or a long-cooking vegetable. If the rice is done a bit before the rest of the meal, simply turn off the heat and let it sit. The cooking plans also remind you to preheat the broiler or oven and to heat water for pasta or for steaming vegetables. The plans are a real boon to the cook in a hurry.

All the photographs throughout this chapter offer ideas for garnishing and serving foods attractively. But most of all, they set the stage for enjoyable, relaxed dining — one of the primary motivations for adopting the quick-cooking techniques described in this book.

Quick-cooking methods such as sauté are basic to 30-minute meals. In a large skillet or sauté pan, you can both cook and serve almost any food including shrimp, as shown here.

1

Sole with Lemon-Butter Sauce and Grapes

Saffron Rice

Zesty Zucchini Sauté

Wine suggestion:
Johannisberg Riesling

Sole with Lemon-Butter Sauce and Grapes

You can use other fish fillets in place of sole, but thicker fillets will need to cook a bit longer. When the fillets are ready to be turned, the edges of the first side will become opaque and curl slightly. When done, the second side should flake easily when prodded with a fork.

- 1¼ pounds sole fillets
- ½ cup flour seasoned with ¼ teaspoon salt and ⅛ teaspoon pepper
- 1 tablespoon *each* butter and oil
- ¼ cup *each* butter, lemon juice, and minced fresh parsley
- 1 cup seedless grapes

1. Dredge fillets in seasoned flour.

2. Heat oven to 200°F and warm serving platter.

3. In a large frying pan over medium-high heat, melt the 1 tablespoon butter with the oil. Without crowding pan, sauté the fillets, rounded side first, until a deep golden color (about 1½ minutes per side). Remove to platter and place in oven.

4. Wipe out pan, return to heat, and add the ¼ cup butter. When it is light brown, add lemon juice, parsley, and grapes. Swirl 1 minute (to heat grapes) and pour sauce over fish.

VARIATIONS

Fillets Amandine

Sauté 2 to 3 tablespoons sliced almonds in 1 tablespoon butter until golden. Add 2 to 3 tablespoons dry vermouth, white wine, *or* Marsala and heat briefly. Pour over sautéed fillets.

Parmesan Fillets with Bananas

Dredge fillets in ¼ cup *each* flour and freshly grated Parmesan cheese. Sauté. In 2 tablespoons butter, sauté 2 sliced bananas. Add 1 tablespoon *each* lemon juice and minced parsley, heat, and spoon over fillets.

Note: Sliced mango or papaya can be substituted for the bananas.

Dilled Fillets with Cucumber

Remove peel in alternate strips from an English *or* a regular cucumber; slice cucumber thinly. Sauté in 2 to 3 tablespoons butter with 1 tablespoon fresh *or* 1 teaspoon dried dill weed. Spoon over sautéed fillets.

Fillets Provençal

In 2 to 3 tablespoons butter, sauté 2 minced cloves garlic, 1 thinly sliced zucchini, and 1 chopped ripe tomato for 5 to 7 minutes. Sprinkle ¼ teaspoon dried basil over surface and stir. For texture, mix in 2 tablespoons browned bread crumbs before spooning over fish.

Fillets with Herbed Yogurt

Mix together ½ cup low-fat yogurt; 2 tablespoons dry white wine; 1 egg yolk; 1 chopped green onion; 1 minced clove garlic; 3 tablespoons minced parsley; and ¼ teaspoon *each* dried thyme, basil, and oregano. Heat through and spread over sautéed fillets.

Saffron Rice

- 2 cups water
- ½ teaspoon salt
- 1/16 teaspoon saffron *or* ⅛ teaspoon turmeric
- 1 cup white rice

Bring all ingredients to a boil. Cover, reduce heat, and simmer until all water is absorbed (20 minutes).

Zesty Zucchini Sauté

- 2 tablespoons *each* butter and oil
- 1 pound zucchini, sliced ⅛ inch thick
- 2 cloves garlic, minced
- 2 tablespoons minced fresh parsley
- 1 tablespoon fresh *or* ½ to 1 teaspoon dried basil
  Salt and freshly ground pepper

1. In a large skillet over medium-high heat, melt butter and oil. When a few drops of water dance in the pan, add zucchini, garlic, parsley, and basil.

2. Sauté, shaking skillet and tossing slices gently with a spatula, until tender-crisp (7 minutes). Season to taste.

C O O K I N G   P L A N

1. Assemble all ingredients and cooking equipment.

2. Start rice.

3. Wash grapes and mince parsley for fish. Slice zucchini; mince parsley and fresh basil. Mix seasoned flour.

4. Sauté zucchini.

5. Heat oven to 200°F and warm platter for fillets.

6. Coat fillets and sauté.

7. Remove fillets to platter and prepare sauce.

To serve: Fluff rice. Pour sauce over fillets and season zucchini.

Above: Minced parsley and seedless green grapes make a piquant finish to the Lemon-Butter Sauce. Right: The sauté technique is great for most types of fish fillets, and you can vary the sauce using the recipes on this page – six dinners in one! Complete the menu with zucchini and the golden saffron rice, or flip through the book for other ideas.

Calamari steaks are truly a "flash-in-the-pan" at 30 to 35 seconds per side. Thin cuts of fish, chicken, or veal cook so quickly that you don't have to start them until 5 minutes before serving. The butter-steamed beans are flavored while they cook.

2

Calamari Steak Sauté

Sauced Spaghetti Squash

Butter-Steamed Green Beans

Wine suggestion:
Australian Cabernet Rosé

Calamari Steak Sauté

Calamari (squid) steaks — also known as poor man's abalone — are new on the market. Any of the sauce variations for Sole with Lemon Butter Sauce and Grapes (page 14) goes well with this 70-second sauté.

- 1 to 1½ pounds calamari steaks
- ½ cup flour seasoned with ⅛ teaspoon *each* dried basil, thyme, and oregano
- 1 egg, lightly beaten with 2 tablespoons milk
- ½ cup bread crumbs
- 2 tablespoons *each* butter and oil Lemon wedges, for garnish

1. Coat steaks with seasoned flour, then with egg-milk mixture, and finally with bread crumbs.

2. Heat oven to 200°F.

3. Heat butter and oil in a wide frying pan. Without crowding, sauté calamari steaks (a few at a time) 30 to 35 seconds per side, adding more butter as needed. Keep steaks warm in oven as sautéed.

4. Garnish with lemon wedges before serving.

Sauced Spaghetti Squash

- 1 spaghetti squash (about 4 lbs) Boiling water
- 1 jar (15½ oz) or 2 cups favorite spaghetti sauce, heated Freshly grated Parmesan cheese

1. Wash squash and cut into quarters. Remove seeds.

2. In enough boiling water to cover, cook squash over medium-high heat, covered, until tender (20 minutes). Drain.

3. Remove pulp from rind by shredding pulp with a fork.

4. Top with heated sauce and Parmesan cheese.

Butter-Steamed Green Beans

- 1 pound green beans
- 2 tablespoons butter
- 5 tablespoons water Salt and freshly ground pepper

1. Wash, trim, and slice beans diagonally into 1-inch lengths.

2. Melt butter in a large skillet over medium-high heat. Add beans and water, stir, cover, and steam until tender (7 minutes). Season to taste.

C O O K I N G   P L A N

1. Assemble all ingredients and cooking equipment.

2. Heat water for squash; quarter, seed, and begin to cook.

3. Warm spaghetti sauce over low heat.

4. Wash and slice beans, grate cheese, and cut lemon into wedges.

5. Mix seasoned flour and coat calamari steaks.

6. Butter-steam beans.

7. Heat oven to 200°F.

8. Sauté calamari steaks; keep warm in oven.

9. Drain and shred squash.

To serve: Top squash with sauce and cheese. Garnish calamari with lemon, and serve beans.

3 Seafood with Kiwi

Shredded Squash

Savory Mushroom Salad
with Poppy Seed Dressing

Poppy and Sesame Seed Rolls

Wine suggestion:
Johannisberg Riesling

Seafood with Kiwi

- 2 tablespoons *each* butter and oil
- 1 to 3 cloves garlic, minced *or* pressed
- ½ to ¾ pound cleaned raw medium-size shrimp
- ¾ pound halibut, cut in 1-inch pieces
- 2 kiwi fruit, peeled and sliced
- ¼ cup *each* lemon juice and minced fresh parsley
- 4 lemon wheels, for garnish (optional)

1. In a large skillet heat butter and oil over medium heat. Add garlic, shrimp, and halibut; sauté until shrimp just begin to turn pink and halibut becomes opaque (4 minutes).

2. Push seafood to edges of pan and warm kiwi briefly in center.

3. All at once, add lemon juice and parsley. Shake skillet a few times to distribute juice. Gently mix fruit and seafood.

4. Garnish with lemon wheels if desired.

VARIATION

Fillets with Fruit
Substitute 1 to 1½ pounds fillets of any white fish for the shrimp and halibut. Sauté 2 to 4 minutes per side. Substitute 2 sliced nectarines, 1 sliced papaya, *or* segments of 1 orange and 1 grapefruit for the kiwi.

Shredded Squash

- 3 medium zucchini squash
- 3 medium yellow crookneck squash
- 2 tablespoons butter
- 1 to 2 cloves garlic, minced *or* pressed
  Freshly grated Parmesan cheese, for garnish

1. Rinse, dry, and shred squash.

2. Melt butter in a large skillet over medium-high heat. Add garlic and sauté until golden.

3. Add squash and sauté, tossing with a spatula to cook evenly (2 to 3 minutes).

4. Garnish with cheese before serving.

The sweet-tartness of kiwi and lemon offer a tantalizing contrast to the delicate seafood, and you'll find that even with 3 cloves, the garlic is not overwhelming. For variety and economy, try any white fish fillets with nectarines, papayas, or mangos.

Savory Mushroom Salad with Poppy Seed Dressing

- 4 large *or* 8 medium mushrooms, sliced
  Half a small red onion, sliced and separated into rings
- 1 bunch watercress, tough stems removed
  Poppy Seed Dressing (recipe follows)

Arrange mushrooms and onion rings on a bed of watercress. Top with dressing.

Poppy Seed Dressing

- ¼ cup *each* honey and lemon juice
- ¾ cup walnut *or* safflower oil
- 1 tablespoon Dijon-style mustard
- 1 green onion, minced
- 1 tablespoon poppy seed
- ½ teaspoon salt

Thoroughly combine all ingredients.

Poppy and Sesame Seed Rolls

Warm 4 to 6 purchased rolls in a 350°F oven for 10 minutes.

COOKING PLAN

1. Assemble all ingredients and cooking equipment.

2. Shred squash, mince garlic, and grate cheese. Make salad and dressing.

3. Mince, chop, and slice ingredients for seafood dish.

4. Place rolls in 350°F oven.

5. Sauté seafood.

6. Sauté squash.

7. Add kiwi to seafood and make sauce.

To serve: Dress salad. Garnish seafood with lemon and squash with cheese.

4

Italian-Style Sea Bass

Spinach Pasta

Red-and-Green Salad

Wine suggestion:
Gamay Rosé or French Tavel

Spinach pasta and a crimson and green salad bring out the colors of the pepper-tomato sauce that tops the bass. Color plays an important role in any meal, and you can use it in both subtle and dramatic ways. Even something as simple as a red rose repeats the colors of the food and adds a special touch. You don't have to have an infinite variety of china and flatware to vary the presentation of food — inexpensive napkins, tablecloths, placemats, napkin rings, small bud vases, baskets, and flowers can all be used to add flair.

Italian-Style Sea Bass

In addition to sea bass, you can prepare this dish with fillets of perch, flounder, snapper, or turbot.

  1 tablespoon olive oil
  1 clove garlic, minced
  ¼ cup *each* seeded and chopped green pepper and chopped onion
  1 can (8 oz) stewed tomatoes
  1 tablespoon lemon juice
  1 teaspoon dried *or* 1 tablespoon chopped fresh basil or oregano
  4 sea bass fillets (1 to 1½ lbs fish)

1. Preheat oven to 350°F.

2. Heat oil and sauté garlic, pepper, and onion until softened. Add tomatoes (breaking up with a fork), lemon juice, and basil and heat through.

3. Place fillets in single layer in a shallow oven-to-table baking dish. Pour sauce over fish and cover with foil.

4. Bake until fish flakes easily when prodded with a fork (15 to 20 minutes).

Spinach Pasta

  2 quarts water
  1 teaspoon salt
  8 ounces green (spinach) pasta
  1 tablespoon oil

1. Bring salted water to a boil.

2. Add pasta and oil and cook, uncovered, until tender but firm (5 to 8 minutes for medium-width noodles). Drain.

3. Spoon some of the fish sauce over pasta before serving.

Red-and-Green Salad

  1 small cucumber, peeled in alternate strips and sliced
  10 to 15 cherry tomatoes, halved
  ½ green onion (halved lengthwise), minced
    Cruets of vinegar and oil

1. Top cucumbers and tomatoes with onion. Allow to remain at room temperature until serving.

2. Accompany with cruets of vinegar and oil or serve with your favorite bottled Italian dressing.

COOKING PLAN

1. Assemble all ingredients and cooking equipment.

2. Preheat oven to 350°F.

3. Wash and chop vegetables for fish.

4. Prepare sauce for fish, assemble dish, and put in oven.

5. Start water for pasta.

6. Slice salad vegetables and assemble salad.

7. Add pasta to boiling water.

8. Check fish; if it flakes easily, it is done.

9. Drain pasta.

To serve: Place cruets and salad on table. Remove fish from oven and spoon some of the sauce over the pasta.

5

Mexicali Fish

Lemon-Lime Rice

Spicy Mexican Corn

Wine suggestion:
Chenin Blanc or Vouvray

Mexicali Fish

Fish fillets bake in their own foil packets,
and juices combine with the authentic
Mexican additions for a self-made sauce.
The almonds add a nice crunch.

    Juice of 1 lime
  1 tablespoon cornstarch
  ⅓ cup white wine, clam juice, or water
  4 snapper, cod, sea bass, or sole fillets
    (1 to 1½ lbs fish)
    Several sprigs of cilantro, washed
  ¼ to ⅓ cup sliced almonds
  1 lime, cut in wedges

1. Preheat oven to 450°F.

2. In a small saucepan, combine lime
juice and cornstarch. Blend in wine and
cook, stirring, over medium-high heat until
thickened.

3. Place each fillet on a piece of foil
large enough to wrap it completely. Top
with 1 or 2 sprigs of cilantro and ¼ of the
almonds.

4. Divide sauce evenly among fillets.
Wrap packets, folding over at edges to
seal, and arrange on a baking sheet.
Bake until fish flakes easily (10 to 12
minutes).

5. Open packets and garnish with lime
wedges before serving.

Lemon-Lime Rice

Citrus-flavored rice is a refreshing contrast
to the other spicy dishes in this menu. For
a more piquant flavor, add a little grated
lemon and lime peel to the water in
which the rice is cooked.

  2 cups water
  ½ teaspoon salt
  1 cup white rice
  2 tablespoons *each* lemon and
    lime juice
  ½ cup minced fresh parsley (optional)

1. Bring water, salt, and rice to a boil.
Cover, reduce heat, and simmer until all
water is absorbed (20 minutes).

2. Mix in juice and parsley before
serving.

Cilantro (fresh coriander or Chinese parsley) and almonds are common partners in Mexican
fish cookery and colorful additions give the corn a spicy flavor as well as a fiesta touch.

Spicy Mexican Corn

Make this colorful, low-calorie vegetable
dish from staples you have on hand.

  1 package (10 oz) frozen corn
  2 tablespoons water
  1 can (4 oz) diced green chiles,
    drained
  1 to 2 tablespoons hot salsa
  1 jar (2 oz) pimientos, diced or in strips

1. In a covered saucepan over low to
medium heat, cook corn until it begins to
thaw (5 minutes).

2. Break up with a fork, add remaining
ingredients, increase heat, and cook until
corn is tender (8 to 10 minutes).

C O O K I N G   P L A N

1. Assemble all ingredients and cooking
equipment.

2. Preheat oven to 450°F.

3. Start rice.

4. Juice lime and prepare sauce for fish.

5. Begin cooking corn.

6. Assemble fish packets and place in
oven.

7. Add remaining ingredients to corn.

8. Measure or squeeze juice and mince
parsley for rice. Cut lime into wedges for
fish.

9. Check fish; if it flakes easily, it is done.

To serve: Add juice and parsley to rice.
Open fish packets and garnish with lime.
Serve corn.

A mélange of vegetables of various shapes and textures is an eye-catching addition to this French Provincial meal featuring fresh, whole rainbow trout garnished with almonds.

Sautéed Vegetable Medley

    Boiling water
1 teaspoon salt
¾ pound small new potatoes, quartered
1 large carrot, cut in sticks
4 small white onions, peeled and halved
½ pound (about 15 medium) mushrooms, halved
2 tablespoons butter
1 teaspoon *each* lemon juice and dried basil
    Grated Parmesan, Romano, *or* Sapsago cheese, for garnish (optional)

1. In enough boiling, salted water to cover, cook potatoes until tender (10 minutes). After 5 minutes, add carrot and onions.

2. Meanwhile, sauté mushrooms in butter in a large skillet.

3. Drain boiled vegetables and sauté briefly with mushrooms.

4. Add lemon juice and basil; toss vegetables to mix. Garnish with cheese if desired.

French Loaf

Warm purchased French loaf in 200°F oven for 15 minutes, or serve at room temperature.

C O O K I N G   P L A N

1. Assemble all ingredients and cooking equipment.

2. Heat water for vegetables.

3. Wash and cut up potatoes, carrot, onions, and mushrooms. Add potatoes to water.

4. Warm bread and platter for fish in 200°F oven.

5. Sauté trout.

6. Add carrots and onions to potatoes; sauté mushrooms.

7. Turn trout.

8. Drain vegetables; sauté with mushrooms.

9. Remove trout to platter and prepare sauce.

10. Add juice and basil to vegetables.

To serve: Remove bread from oven. Toss vegetables and pour sauce over trout.

6

Trout with Almonds

Sautéed Vegetable Medley

French Loaf

Wine suggestion:
Gewürztraminer or Chenin Blanc

Trout with Almonds

Golden sautéed almonds are a crisp, flavorful contrast to the delicate trout. You can use almost any small whole fish in this recipe.

4 medium-size trout, cleaned
    Lemon juice
    Freshly cracked black pepper
2 tablespoons *each* butter and oil
¼ cup butter
½ cup sliced almonds
¼ cup *each* lemon juice *or* white wine and minced fresh parsley

1. Rub trout with lemon juice and pepper.

2. Warm platter for fish in 200°F oven.

3. Heat the 2 tablespoons butter and oil in a wide frying pan over medium-high heat. (Use 2 pans if necessary.) Add trout

and sauté until lightly browned on one side. Turn when edges become opaque and curl slightly (3 to 5 minutes). The second side is done when fish flakes when prodded with a fork at the thickest portion near the backbone. Remove fish to warm platter.

4. Wipe out pan and melt the ¼ cup butter. Add almonds and sauté until golden.

5. Add lemon juice and parsley all at once. Swirl and pour sauce over trout.

VARIATIONS

Sauté trout as directed in Step 3 and wipe out pan.

Trout with Meunière Sauce

Melt ¼ cup butter. Add ¼ cup *each* lemon juice and minced fresh parsley; swirl and pour over trout. Garnish with fresh or canned pineapple slices if desired.

Trout with Lemon-Dill Sauce

In ¼ cup butter, sauté 2 minced shallots *or* 2 tablespoons yellow onion. Add ¼ cup dry sherry, finely grated peel of 1 lemon, and 4 minced sprigs fresh dill *or* fennel (or 1 teaspoon dried). Swirl and pour over trout.

This light dinner is pure simplicity. Buttery broiled salmon can stand on its own, or you can top it with the Lemon Mayonnaise on page 46. The placement of the tomato is a small but special touch. Serve with Herbed Cauliflower or Fresh Buttered Asparagus (page 39).

7

Broiled Salmon Steaks

Herbed Cauliflower

Tomatoes au Gratin

Wine suggestion:
White Bordeaux

Broiled Salmon Steaks

  4 salmon steaks, *each* ¾ inch thick
  ¼ cup melted butter
  1 teaspoon dried marjoram
    Salt and freshly ground pepper

1. Preheat broiler.

2. Brush salmon steaks well with butter on both sides. Sprinkle both sides of fish with marjoram and salt and pepper to taste.

3. On oiled rack 4 inches from heat source, broil steaks until first side is lightly browned (5 to 8 minutes). Baste with butter, turn, baste again, and broil 5 to 8 minutes longer or until fish flakes easily when prodded with a fork.

Herbed Cauliflower

  2 tablespoons butter
  1 medium head cauliflower, divided into flowerets
  5 tablespoons water
  1 tablespoon chopped fresh *or* 1 teaspoon dried tarragon
    Salt and freshly ground pepper
  ¼ cup shredded Muenster cheese (optional)

1. Melt butter in large skillet over medium-high heat. Add cauliflower and water, stir, cover, and steam until tender (7 to 10 minutes).

2. Toss with tarragon, season to taste, and top with cheese if desired.

Tomatoes au Gratin

Fluted or halved tomatoes are attractive when served in the hollows of the salmon steaks.

  2 large tomatoes, halved *or* fluted
  2 tablespoons melted butter
  ½ cup freshly grated Parmesan *or* Romano cheese
  ¼ cup bread *or* cracker crumbs
  2 tablespoons dry white wine, tomato juice, *or* chicken broth
  ½ teaspoon *each* paprika and basil

1. Squeeze tomato halves gently to remove seeds.

2. Combine remaining ingredients and divide evenly among tomato halves, pressing lightly into tomatoes.

3. Broil on oiled foil with salmon during last 10 minutes.

C O O K I N G   P L A N

1. Assemble all ingredients and cooking equipment.

2. Preheat broiler.

3. Melt butter for salmon. Halve tomatoes and grate cheese. Wash and separate cauliflower.

4. Brush salmon with butter and season. Place under broiler.

5. Assemble tomatoes and place in broiler. Cook cauliflower.

6. Turn salmon.

To serve: Toss cauliflower with seasonings. Remove salmon and tomatoes from broiler and place tomatoes in hollows of salmon steaks.

8

Scallops in Wine Sauce

Squash and Mushrooms with Herbs

Cheesy Baguette Rounds

Wine suggestion:
White Burgundy

These scallops are poached in a court bouillon of wine and herbs. Bite-size chunks of any fish fillets can be substituted for or added to the scallops to reduce the cost.

Scallops in Wine Sauce

- ¼ cup chicken *or* clam broth
- ¼ cup white wine
- ¼ cup finely chopped green onion *or* 2 shallots, minced
- ½ teaspoon dried tarragon *or* herb of choice
- 1 to 1½ pounds scallops, cut in half
- 2 tablespoons *each* butter and flour
- ¼ cup freshly grated Parmesan cheese
  Minced fresh chives, for garnish

1. Preheat broiler.

2. In a large skillet, bring broth, wine, onion, and tarragon to a boil.

3. Reduce heat to a simmer, add scallops, cover, and cook until scallops become opaque (5 minutes). Remove to ovenproof serving dish, reserving liquid.

4. In a small saucepan, melt butter over medium heat, stir in flour, and cook until bubbly. Add reserved fish broth and cook until sauce thickens.

5. Pour sauce over scallops, sprinkle with Parmesan cheese, and place under broiler until lightly browned (2 to 3 minutes). Garnish with chives.

VARIATIONS

Scallops Meunière

Sauté scallops in 4 tablespoons butter until opaque. Add ¼ cup *each* lemon juice and minced fresh parsley.

Scallops Amandine

Sauté scallops in 4 tablespoons butter. In separate skillet, sauté 4 tablespoons sliced *or* slivered almonds in 2 tablespoons butter. Add ¼ cup white wine *or* Marsala and 1 to 2 tablespoons Cognac *or* brandy. Pour over scallops.

Sweet-and-Sour Scallops

Heat ½ cup pineapple juice, 2 tablespoons *each* butter and brown sugar, 1 to 2 teaspoons soy sauce, ½ teaspoon pepper, ¼ cup mild vinegar, and 1 teaspoon grated ginger root. Add scallops and simmer until they become opaque.

Squash and Mushrooms with Herbs

- 1 pound (4 small) crookneck *or* zucchini squash
- ½ pound (20 medium) mushrooms
- ¼ cup chicken broth
- ½ teaspoon dried basil *or* tarragon
  Salt and freshly ground pepper

1. Trim ends of squash and quarter. Halve mushrooms.

2. Place in skillet with remaining ingredients, cover, and simmer until tender-crisp (6 to 8 minutes).

Cheesy Baguette Rounds

- ½ cup (1 cube) butter, softened
- ¼ cup freshly grated Parmesan cheese
- 1 teaspoon lemon juice (optional)
- 2 to 3 cloves garlic, minced *or* pressed
- 2 tablespoons chopped fresh watercress *or* parsley
  Baguette, cut in 1-inch-thick slices

1. Combine all ingredients except baguette.

2. Spread on slices and broil until golden (3 minutes).

C O O K I N G   P L A N

1. Assemble all ingredients and cooking equipment.

2. Cut up, chop, and grate ingredients for all dishes.

3. Prepare seasoned butter, slice bread, and spread slices with butter.

4. Preheat broiler.

5. Bring broth to a boil; add scallops.

6. Cook squash and mushrooms.

7. Make sauce for scallops and assemble dish.

8. Place scallops and bread in broiler.

To serve: Remove bread and scallops from broiler. Garnish scallops and serve squash.

9

Shrimp and Scallops in Shells

Herbed Rice and Peas

Wine suggestion:
White Burgundy or Pinot Blanc

Shrimp and Scallops in Shells

This menu is light, and the sauce for the the seafood is low in both calories and cholesterol. If you don't have the traditional scallop shells, use ramekins, or individual 1-cup casseroles.

- 3 cups nonfat dry milk
- ¼ cup cornstarch
- 1 teaspoon salt
- ½ teaspoon *Fine Herbes* (or pinch *each* parsley, chives, tarragon, and chervil)
- 2 cups hot water
- ¼ cup safflower oil
- ½ cup shredded Monterey jack cheese
- 1 teaspoon butter
- ½ pound (20 medium) mushrooms, sliced
- ¼ cup *each* vermouth and dry sherry
- ½ pound scallops, cut in half
- ½ pound fresh *or* frozen small cleaned shrimp
- ½ cup shredded Monterey jack cheese
- ¼ cup bread crumbs

1. Preheat oven to 450°F, and heat water in bottom of double boiler.

2. In top of double boiler, combine milk, cornstarch, salt, and herbs. Blend in water and oil.

3. Cook over rapidly boiling water, stirring often. When mixture thickens and begins to bubble, stir in the ½ cup cheese.

4. Meanwhile, in a skillet, melt butter and sauté mushrooms until barely tender. Remove from pan.

5. Add vermouth and sherry to skillet. Bring to a boil, reduce heat, and add scallops. Cook over medium-low heat until opaque (3 to 4 minutes). Add shrimp during last minute to warm.

6. Fold scallops, shrimp, cooking liquid, and mushrooms into sauce in double boiler.

7. Spoon mixture evenly into 4 shells. Sprinkle with the ½ cup cheese and the bread crumbs.

8. Bake, uncovered, at 450°F until sauce bubbles (5 to 8 minutes).

Enveloped in a richly flavored sherried sauce and served in pretty shells, these two seafood favorites—shrimp and scallops—make a delicious special-occasion meal.

Herbed Rice and Peas

- 1½ cups water
- ½ cup white wine *or* an additional ½ cup water
- 2 teaspoons lemon juice
- ½ teaspoon salt
- 1 teaspoon *each* dried basil and thyme
- 1 cup white rice
- 3 tablespoons minced fresh parsley Half a 20-ounce bag frozen petite peas

1. Bring all ingredients (except parsley and peas) to a boil, reduce heat, cover, and simmer 15 minutes.

2. Quickly add parsley and peas (do *not* stir into rice), cover, and cook until all liquid is absorbed and peas are hot (about 5 minutes).

3. Mix peas and parsley into rice before serving.

C O O K I N G P L A N

1. Assemble all ingredients and cooking equipment.

2. Preheat oven to 450°F; heat water in bottom of double boiler.

3. Remove peas from package to thaw slightly. Begin rice.

4. Cut up scallops, slice mushrooms, and grate cheese; measure other ingredients for seafood. Mince parsley for rice.

5. In double boiler, prepare sauce for seafood.

6. Sauté mushrooms. Poach scallops. Add shrimp briefly.

7. Add parsley and peas to rice.

8. Combine seafood, mushrooms, and sauce; spoon into shells. Add topping and place in oven.

To serve: Remove scallops from oven. Toss rice to mix ingredients, and serve.

10

Halibut with Almond Butter

Fresh Broccoli Purée
in Fluted Tomato Halves

Crusty Baguette or French Bread

Wine suggestion:
German Riesling

Halibut with Almond Butter

For variety, try preparing swordfish or skate wings in this manner. All of the sauce variations given with Menu 1 (page 14) are also compatible with halibut.

- ½ cup (1 cube) sweet butter
- 1 package (3½ oz) sliced or slivered almonds
- 2 to 3 tablespoons lemon juice
- 1 tablespoon chopped fresh parsley
  Dash Worcestershire sauce
- 4 halibut steaks or fillets (about 1½ lbs fish)
  Sliced almonds and lemon wedges, for garnish

1. Preheat broiler.

2. Melt ¼ cup (½ cube) of the butter in a small skillet over medium heat. (Cut the remainder in 4 pieces and set aside to soften.) Cook until foamy and light brown. Add almonds and sauté until lightly toasted. Place in blender or food processor, add next 3 ingredients and the softened butter, and blend or process 10 seconds. Remove from container and chill.

3. Broil halibut 4 inches from heat source until first side is lightly browned (3 to 5 minutes). Turn and broil until fish flakes easily when prodded with a fork (3 to 5 minutes more).

4. To serve, dollop 2 tablespoons almond butter on each steak. Sprinkle with almonds and garnish with lemon wedges.

Fresh Broccoli Purée in Fluted Tomato Halves

Water for steaming
- 1 bunch broccoli (2 lbs), roughly chopped
- 2 large tomatoes
- ½ to ¾ cup ricotta cheese, plain yogurt, or sour cream
- 1 tablespoon lemon juice
  Dash nutmeg, salt, and freshly ground pepper
  Parmesan cheese, for garnish (optional)

1. Over boiling water, steam broccoli until tender (10 to 15 minutes).

2. Flute tomatoes by cutting in half using a sawtooth pattern. Twist to separate halves. Gently squeeze out seeds. Set aside.

3. In a blender or processor, purée broccoli with ricotta. Season to taste.

4. Fill each tomato half with purée and serve on a bed of purée. Garnish with cheese if desired.

Crusty Baguette or French Bread

After removing fish from broiler, turn off heat and warm bread briefly in oven, or serve at room temperature.

C O O K I N G   P L A N

1. Assemble all ingredients and cooking equipment.

2. Heat water for broccoli and melt butter for almonds.

3. Mince parsley for almond butter. Wash and chop broccoli; add to steamer.

4. Heat broiler.

5. Toast almonds and flute tomatoes.

6. Prepare almond butter, remove from blender or processor, and chill. (It's not necessary to wash container before puréeing broccoli.)

7. Broil halibut.

8. Purée broccoli. Turn halibut.

9. When halibut is done, turn off broiler and warm bread in oven.

To serve: Fill tomatoes with purée; serve remainder underneath. Dot halibut with almond butter, and garnish. Remove bread from oven.

A dollop of this Worcestershire-flavored almond butter is a quick way to add zest to a mildly flavored fish such as halibut. And, simply by puréeing broccoli and serving it with fluted tomatoes, two humble vegetables become edible art, dramatizing an elegant meal.

11

Chicken with Mushrooms

Fresh-Herb Pasta

Carrots Vichy

Wine suggestion:
Fumé or Sauvignon Blanc

Chicken with Mushrooms

- 8 boned chicken breast halves
- 1 tablespoon *each* butter and oil
- 2 cloves garlic, minced *or* pressed
- 3 to 4 green onions, sliced
- 1 cup sliced fresh mushrooms
- ⅓ cup Madeira wine
  Minced fresh parsley, for garnish (optional)

1. Pound breasts to a thickness of ¼ inch, to speed cooking.

2. Heat butter and oil in 2 wide sauté pans over medium-high heat. Add breasts, skin side down. Add garlic, onions, and mushrooms to one of the pans. Sauté until chicken is lightly browned (3 to 5 minutes per side) and vegetables are tender.

3. Add Madeira to pan with vegetables, shaking pan to distribute, heat, and ignite. (If necessary, chicken and sauce can be covered and kept warm in a 200°F oven until served.) Garnish with parsley if desired.

⌐ VARIATIONS

Sauté chicken as directed in Step 2, but omit vegetables. Top with one of the following sauces.

Chicken Amandine

In a separate small skillet, sauté 1 minced clove garlic in 1 tablespoon butter. Add ½ cup sliced almonds and sauté until golden. Add ¼ cup Marsala, port, *or* dry sherry; swirl; and ignite. Pour sauce over chicken.

Chicken Rosemary

While chicken sautés, add 2 to 3 minced cloves garlic and 1 tablespoon minced fresh *or* ½ teaspoon dried, crushed rosemary leaves.

Chicken Veronique

Just before serving, add ⅓ cup *each* lemon juice *or* dry white wine and whipping cream. Bring to a boil and cook until slightly thickened. Stir in 1 cup grapes.

Chicken breasts are ideal for a speedy sauté, and for a little kitchen showmanship, heat the Madeira for a flambé finish. With different sauces, chicken takes on new personalities. Be sure to try all the delicious sauce ideas on this page.

Lemon Chicken

In a small saucepan, melt 2 tablespoons butter. Add 2 tablespoons flour, 2 to 3 cloves minced garlic, and 1 tablespoon grated lemon *or* orange peel (or 1½ teaspoons *each*). Cook over medium-high heat until bubbly. Stir in ½ cup dry white wine and cook until thickened. Pour sauce over chicken and garnish with minced parsley and lemon wheels.

Fresh-Herb Pasta

- 2 quarts water
- 1 teaspoon salt
- 8 ounces wide *or* medium noodles
- 1 tablespoon oil
  Freshly ground black pepper
- 2 tablespoons chopped fresh rosemary, thyme, *or* chives

1. Bring salted water to a boil, add noodles and oil, and cook until tender but firm (5 to 8 minutes). Drain.

2. Toss with pepper and herb before serving.

Carrots Vichy

- 16 baby carrots, scrubbed and trimmed
  Boiling salted water
- ¼ cup butter
- 2 tablespoons brandy *or* lemon juice
- 1 tablespoon brown sugar *or* honey

1. Place carrots in a large frying pan in the water. Cover and simmer until tender-crisp (10 to 15 minutes). Do not overcook. Drain.

2. Push carrots to one side and add butter, brandy, and sugar, stirring to combine. Sauté carrots over medium-high heat, shaking pan, until carrots are well coated and lightly browned.

C O O K I N G P L A N

1. Assemble all ingredients and cooking equipment.

2. Pound breasts.

3. Mince and slice ingredients for chicken. Mince herb for pasta. Scrub carrots.

4. Heat water for pasta.

5. Begin cooking carrots.

6. Sauté chicken.

7. Add pasta to boiling water.

8. Turn chicken.

9. Drain carrots and prepare glaze.

To serve: Drain pasta and toss with herb. Garnish chicken and serve carrots.

Parmesan Chicken Breasts Sauté

Braised Celery with Walnuts

Minted Carrots

Wine suggestion:
Italian Frascati

Pounded chicken breasts cook quickly and easily, and while they're sautéing, you can chop up all the ingredients for the two vegetable dishes. Having everything out and ready allows you to bring preparation to a smooth and timely finish.

Parmesan Chicken Breasts Sauté

- 8 boned and skinned chicken breast halves
- ½ cup flour
- 1 egg, lightly beaten with 2 tablespoons water
- ¼ cup *each* seasoned bread crumbs and Parmesan cheese
- 2 tablespoons *each* butter and oil
  Grapes and mandarin orange segments warmed in a little of the mandarin juice *or* sliced avocado and citrus fruit, for garnish

1. Pound breasts to a thickness of ¼ inch.

2. Place flour, egg, and crumb-cheese mixture in individual shallow dishes. Coat chicken, in that order, and place on a large platter.

3. Preheat oven to 200°F.

4. Heat butter and oil in a wide frying pan and sauté half the breasts until golden (3 to 5 minutes per side). Do not crowd pan. Keep cooked breasts warm in oven while sautéing remaining breasts. Add more butter as needed.

5. Garnish as desired.

VARIATIONS

Citrus Chicken

Omit Parmesan cheese from breading mix and increase bread crumbs to ½ cup. Add 1 tablespoon *each* grated orange and lemon peel to bread crumbs. Garnish with fruit wheels.

Chicken in Cream

Coat chicken with ½ cup flour mixed with ¼ cup Parmesan cheese. Sauté as directed. Then pour around it: ½ cup whipping cream, 1 tablespoon Dijon-style mustard, and ¾ cup sliced fresh mushrooms. Simmer 5 to 10 minutes. Remove chicken and reduce sauce by boiling. Just before serving, stir in ½ cup shredded Swiss cheese and 2 table-spoons minced green onion.

Braised Celery with Walnuts

- 1 head celery, separated into stalks and washed
  Boiling salted water
- 1 small onion, finely chopped
- ⅓ cup coarsely chopped walnuts
- 2 tablespoons butter
  Grated peel of 1 lemon

1. Cut celery diagonally into 1½-inch pieces.

2. Add to boiling water and blanch 5 minutes. Drain.

3. Meanwhile, in a large skillet, sauté onion and walnuts in butter. Add lemon peel and celery. Toss to coat celery.

Minted Carrots

- 2 tablespoons butter
- 3 cups thinly sliced carrots (10 to 12 slender carrots)
- ¼ cup water
- 2 tablespoons chopped fresh *or* 2 teaspoons dried mint
  Salt and freshly ground pepper

1. In a large frying pan, melt butter over high heat. Add carrots and water, cover, and cook until liquid evaporates (5 to 8 minutes). Stir occasionally.

2. Stir in mint and season to taste.

COOKING PLAN

1. Assemble all ingredients and cooking equipment.

2. Heat oven to 200°F.

3. Pound breasts. Prepare coating mixtures. Dredge breasts and sauté 4 of them.

4. Wash and slice celery, chop onion, and grate lemon peel. Slice carrots and chop mint.

5. Keep cooked breasts warm in oven; sauté second 4.

6. Heat water for celery; blanch.

7. Cook carrots.

8. Sauté flavorings for celery and prepare garnish for chicken.

To serve: Toss carrots and celery with flavorings. Garnish chicken.

After browning on top of the stove, the chicken bakes in the oven along with squash slices while you leisurely prepare the Greek Salad and dressing and heat the rolls. The high heat of both browning and baking cooks the chicken thighs quickly.

13

Chicken Rosemary

Baked Squash Slices

Greek Salad

Bran Muffins

Wine suggestion:
Italian Orvieto or oak-aged Chablis

Chicken Rosemary

To vary the flavor of this dish, substitute basil, oregano, or thyme for the rosemary.

- 8 chicken thighs
- ¼ cup olive oil
  Juice of half a lemon
- 1 tablespoon chopped fresh or 1 teaspoon dried rosemary, crushed
  Salt and freshly ground black pepper, to taste
  Lemon wheels, for garnish

1. Preheat oven to 450°F.

2. In ovenproof casserole or skillet over medium-high heat, sauté chicken, skin side down, until golden (5 minutes).

3. Mix oil, lemon juice, rosemary, and salt and pepper. Turn chicken and pour sauce over. Cover and bake 15 to 20 minutes.

4. Garnish with lemon wheels.

Baked Squash Slices

- 1 small acorn squash
- 1 large zucchini squash
  Olive oil
  Salt and freshly ground pepper

1. Wash both squashes. Halve acorn squash and remove seeds; peel. Cut both squashes into ¼-inch slices and arrange in shallow baking dish.

2. Drizzle oil over squash and season to taste. Cover and bake in 450°F oven with chicken until tender (15 to 20 minutes).

Greek Salad

- 1 head red leaf *or* romaine lettuce
- 2 green onions, chopped
- 1 small cucumber, peeled in alternate strips, quartered lengthwise, and sliced
- 3 ounces feta cheese, crumbled
- 8 to 10 Greek olives
- ¼ cup olive oil
- 3 tablespoons red wine vinegar
  Dash dry mustard
  Cherry tomatoes (optional)

1. Wash and dry greens; chop roughly.

2. Add onions, cucumber, cheese, and olives and toss gently to combine.

3. Whisk together oil, vinegar, and mustard. Pour over salad and toss.

4. Garnish with cherry tomatoes if desired.

Bran Muffins

A slightly sweet roll is a nice change as a supper accompaniment. Bran muffins, purchased from a quality bakery, are quite compatible with the rosemary chicken. Warm in 450°F oven for 5 minutes if desired.

C O O K I N G   P L A N

1. Assemble all ingredients and cooking equipment.

2. Preheat oven to 450°F.

3. Sauté chicken.

4. Meanwhile, clean and slice squash and place in baking dish.

5. Add sauce ingredients to chicken; place chicken and squash in oven.

6. Prepare salad and dressing.

7. Place rolls in oven.

To serve: Toss salad with dressing. Remove rolls, squash, and chicken from oven; garnish chicken.

14

Breast of Chicken à la Reimann

Savory Rice Pilaf

Broccoli Sauté

Wine suggestion:
French Semillon

This rich chicken entrée is a gourmet choice, complete with Cognac and cream and garnished with spring green onions or parsley to complement the celeried rice pilaf.

Breast of Chicken à la Reimann

- 3 whole chicken breasts, skinned and boned
- 3 tablespoons butter
- ¼ cup chopped shallots *or* green onion
- ½ cup slivered almonds, browned in 2 tablespoons butter
- 2 tablespoons flour
- ½ cup white wine *or* chicken broth
- 1 teaspoon tarragon
  Salt and freshly ground pepper
- ¼ cup Cognac *or* brandy
- 1 egg yolk
- ⅓ cup half-and-half
  Chopped green onions, parsley *or* chives, for garnish

1. Cut chicken breasts into ½-inch strips.

2. In a large frying pan over medium-high heat, melt butter. Sauté chicken and shallots just until chicken turns white. (Strips should be pink in centers.) Remove chicken and shallots from pan.

3. Meanwhile, in a small skillet sauté almonds in butter until golden.

4. Add flour to drippings in large frying pan and cook, stirring, until bubbly. Stir in wine and tarragon. Return chicken and shallots to pan and heat 2 to 3 minutes. Season to taste.

5. Add Cognac to pan, heat, and ignite.

6. Beat yolk lightly with half-and-half. Stir gradually into sauce and cook until sauce thickens. (Don't allow sauce to boil after adding yolk or it may curdle.)

7. Fold in almonds and garnish with green onions.

Savory Rice Pilaf

- 2 tablespoons butter
- ⅓ to ½ cup chopped red onion
- 1 cup rice
- 2 cups chicken broth *or* 1 cup *each* water and white wine
- 2 tablespoons minced parsley

1. Melt butter in saucepan and sauté onion until soft and translucent.

2. Add rice and shake pan until rice is well coated with butter.

3. Add stock, bring to a boil, cover, reduce heat, and simmer 20 minutes.

4. A few minutes before rice is done, stir in parsley.

Note: Optional additions to this pilaf include half a bay leaf and ¼ teaspoon paprika added with the broth; ¼ cup sliced fresh mushrooms, celery, pimiento, *or* almonds added 5 minutes before rice is done. Or, substitute minced cilantro or watercress for the parsley.

Broccoli Sauté

- 1 bunch broccoli
  Boiling salted water
- 2 tablespoons butter
- 1 teaspoon lemon juice
- 1 to 2 cloves garlic, minced

1. Wash and chop broccoli, including part of the stalks.

2. In enough boiling water to cover, cook broccoli in covered saucepan until tender-crisp (8 to 10 minutes). Drain and set aside.

3. Melt butter in same saucepan, add garlic, lemon juice, and broccoli and quickly sauté until heated through.

C O O K I N G   P L A N

1. Assemble all ingredients and cooking equipment.

2. Chop onion and start rice.

3. Wash and chop broccoli; mince garlic. Chop shallots and slice chicken. Mince parsley for rice.

4. Sauté chicken and toast almonds.

5. Heat water and add broccoli.

6. Add sauce ingredients to chicken.

7. Heat Cognac and add to chicken.

8. Drain broccoli and sauté.

9. Add egg and cream to chicken.

To serve: Add parsley to rice and fluff. Fold almonds into chicken and garnish. Serve broccoli.

Try this delicious enchilada dish, and then use your imagination to vary toppings, filling, and sauce. Or prepare it in quantity — to serve a crowd or to freeze some for another meal. For other Mexican dishes, see Ortho's book Adventures in Mexican Cooking.

Chicken Enchiladas

Refried Beans

Shredded Lettuce Salad with Salsa

Beverage suggestion:
Sangria or Margaritas

Chicken Enchiladas

This low-cost meal is easy to put together. Serve garnishes — sliced radishes, sliced ripe olives, chopped cilantro or parsley, chopped tomato, and sour cream — in small bowls.

⅓ cup chopped red or yellow onion
1 tablespoon butter
2 cups cooked, shredded chicken
1 can (8 oz) stewed tomatoes
¼ cup hot or mild salsa
  Canned diced green chiles (optional)
¼ to ½ teaspoon chili powder (or to taste)
  Salt and freshly ground pepper
1 can (11 oz) enchilada sauce

8 flour or corn tortillas
¼ cup hot or mild salsa
¾ cup shredded Monterey jack cheese

1. Preheat oven to 450°F.

2. In a large skillet, sauté onion in butter until softened. Add next 6 ingredients and heat through. Keep warm over low heat.

3. Cover the bottom of a 12x8x2-inch baking pan with half the enchilada sauce.

4. One at a time, dampen each tortilla with water and heat on both sides in a hot, ungreased skillet until soft and pliable.

5. Place ¼ cup meat mixture on each tortilla and roll; place in baking dish. Repeat. Top with remaining enchilada sauce, salsa, and cheese.

6. Cover and bake until heated through (15 minutes).

Refried Beans

In a small skillet or saucepan, heat 1 can (16 oz) spicy or regular refried beans. Top with shredded Monterey jack cheese and chopped green onions if desired.

Shredded Lettuce Salad with Salsa

½ head lettuce
1 avocado
½ cup sliced ripe olives
  Salsa

1. Shred lettuce. Peel, seed, and slice avocado.

2. Distribute avocado and olives over lettuce. Top with salsa.

COOKING PLAN

1. Assemble all ingredients and cooking equipment.

2. Chop onion; shred chicken and cheese for enchiladas.

3. Preheat oven to 450°F.

4. Prepare enchilada filling.

5. Warm tortillas and assemble enchiladas. Place in oven.

6. Heat refried beans.

7. Prepare salad and chop garnishes.

To serve: Place garnishes, salad, refried beans, and enchiladas on table.

Carry out the Oriental theme of this menu with nothing more than a placemat and chopsticks. And try using the sauce as a marinade when barbequing red meats.

Wild-and-White Rice

Cook 1 package (6 oz) wild-and-white rice according to package directions (about 25 minutes).

Butter-Steamed Leeks

- 1 bunch leeks
- 2 tablespoons butter
- ¼ cup water
- ¼ cup freshly grated Parmesan cheese

1. Trim leek root ends and remove most of green leaves. Split lengthwise and wash under cold water, separating leaves to clean thoroughly.

2. In a wide frying pan over medium-high heat, melt butter until it browns slightly.

3. Add leeks and the ¼ cup water, cover, and increase heat to high. Cook until tender (3 to 5 minutes). Sprinkle with cheese before serving.

Sautéed Snow Peas

- 1 pound fresh snow peas
- 1 to 2 cloves garlic, minced or pressed
- 1 tablespoon butter
  Salt and freshly ground pepper

1. Wash and drain snow peas; remove ends if desired.

2. In a large frying pan, heat garlic in butter over medium-high heat. Add snow peas, season to taste, and sauté until peas are shiny and heated through (2 to 3 minutes).

C O O K I N G   P L A N

1. Assemble all ingredients and cooking equipment.

2. Start rice.

3. Preheat oven to 450°F.

4. Sauté chicken. Meanwhile, mince garlic and prepare sauce.

5. Put chicken in oven.

6. Clean leeks and grate cheese. Wash peas and mince garlic.

7. Cook leeks.

8. Remove cover from chicken and sauté snow peas.

To serve: Remove chicken from oven; fluff rice. Top leeks with cheese and serve peas.

16

Korean Chicken Thighs

Wild-and-White Rice

Butter-Steamed Leeks

Sautéed Snow Peas

Beverage suggestion:
Sake

Korean Chicken Thighs

- 8 chicken thighs
- 2 tablespoons *each* butter and oil
- 1 cup soy sauce
- ¼ cup sugar
- 2 to 3 cloves garlic, minced or pressed
- ¼ cup red wine *or* white vinegar
- 1½ teaspoons crushed red pepper flakes

1. Preheat oven to 450°F.

2. In a large ovenproof skillet or casserole over medium-high heat, sauté chicken, skin side down, in butter and oil until golden (5 minutes). Drain fat.

3. While chicken is cooking, mix remaining ingredients to create sauce.

4. Turn chicken, pour sauce over, cover, and place in oven. Bake until tender (15 to 20 minutes), removing cover during last 5 minutes to crisp skin.

VARIATIONS

Prepare chicken as directed through Step 2.

Mustard-Sauce Chicken

Mix together 3 tablespoons Dijon-style mustard and 2 tablespoons red wine vinegar. Spread over thighs after turning and bake as directed.

Hawaiian Chicken

Drain 1 can (8 oz) pineapple chunks, reserving ⅔ cup juice. (Use half a fresh pineapple if available.) Distribute pineapple over chicken after turning, top with 2 thinly sliced limes *or* 1 thinly sliced lemon and 1 cup sliced almonds. Pour juice over (fresh pineapple needs no juice) and bake as directed.

Indian Chicken

Add 1 chopped small red onion to chicken while sautéing. Mix together 1 cup plain yogurt, ¼ cup tomato paste, 1 to 2 minced cloves garlic, 2 teaspoons curry powder, ½ teaspoon ground coriander, ¼ teaspoon *each* ground cumin and ginger, and salt and pepper to taste. Spread over chicken after turning and bake as directed.

Moroccan Turkey Sauté

Couscous

Mediterranean Green Bean Salad with Tomatoes

Wine suggestion:
Chenin Blanc

Moroccan Turkey Sauté

Turkey breast, boned and cut into chunks, makes a tender basis for this fragrant, spicy-sweet dish. Accompany it with small bowls of grated coconut, toasted almonds, raisins, chutney, and lemon wedges.

- 2 tablespoons olive oil
- 1 turkey breast (1 to 1½ lbs), cut into 1-inch pieces
- ½ cup chopped green onion
  Half a red or green pepper, seeded and sliced (optional)
- 2 cloves garlic, minced or pressed
- ½ pound (20 medium) mushrooms, sliced
- 1 cup chicken broth
- ½ cup raisins
- 1 to 2 tablespoons brown sugar or honey
- 1 teaspoon each cinnamon, salt, and allspice
- 1½ teaspoons cumin

1. Heat oil in a large skillet and sauté next 5 ingredients, over high heat, 8 to 10 minutes.

2. Add remaining ingredients and heat through (about 8 minutes). Serve alongside couscous.

Couscous

Couscous is a tasty grain that is also quick to cook. To reduce starchiness, try this technique.

- 3 cups chicken broth
- 2 cups couscous

1. Bring broth to a boil and add couscous.

2. Immediately remove from heat, cover, and let stand 5 minutes. Fluff with a fork before serving.

Mediterranean Green Bean Salad with Tomatoes

- 1 pound green beans, trimmed
  Boiling water for steaming
- 1 cup plain yogurt
- 1½ teaspoons cumin
- 2 large tomatoes, sliced

With turkey breasts and these authentic seasonings, you can create a dish that's as tasty as its Middle Eastern lamb equivalent. Mix the dressing with the beans or serve it on top.

1. In a covered steamer, cook beans until fork-tender (10 to 12 minutes).

2. Meanwhile, in a large bowl mix yogurt and cumin. Add cooked, drained beans to dressing and place in freezer to cool quickly. Toss occasionally to cool evenly.

3. To serve, mound beans in center of platter and surround with a ring of tomatoes.

COOKING PLAN

1. Assemble all ingredients and cooking equipment.

2. While heating water for steaming, clean beans. (Trim ends 3 or 4 at a time for speed.) Place in steamer.

3. Cut up turkey and chop onion, garlic, and mushrooms.

4. Begin turkey sauté.

5. Mix dressing for beans; combine with beans and place in freezer.

6. Add remaining ingredients to turkey.

7. Heat broth for couscous.

8. Slice tomatoes and place condiments in bowls.

9. Add couscous to broth; remove from heat.

10. Assemble bean salad.

To serve: Fluff couscous and accompany with turkey and salad.

Ground turkey is a relatively new product on the market that's low in calories, cholesterol, and cost. Mildly flavored by itself, the turkey is transformed into a great Mexican dish with salsa, cumin, and traditional tostada garnishes.

18

Mexican Ground Turkey Pita

Green Leaf and Cilantro Salad

Beverage suggestion:
Mexican beer with lime wedges

Mexican Ground Turkey Pita

Ground turkey makes a lean substitute for ground beef, and this spicy presentation gives it spark. If ground turkey isn't available at your store, ask the butcher to grind turkey parts for you or grind them yourself in a food processor.

- 1 tablespoon butter
- 1 pound ground turkey
- ½ cup chopped red onion
- 3 to 4 tablespoons salsa
- 1 teaspoon dried oregano
- ⅛ teaspoon ground cumin
- ½ teaspoon salt
- ¼ teaspoon freshly ground pepper
- 4 whole pita breads, warmed (see Note)
- 2 cups shredded iceberg lettuce
- 2 medium tomatoes, cut in wedges
  Half a small red onion, thinly sliced
- ¼ cup sour cream or plain yogurt
- 4 ripe olives
  Salsa

1. Melt butter in a large skillet over high heat. Add turkey, breaking up with a fork.

2. Add onion, salsa, and spices and cook until turkey is golden and juices are clear.

3. To assemble individual servings: place a whole pita on each plate. Top with ¼ of the lettuce, turkey, and remaining garnishes, in order listed.

Note: To warm pitas, wrap in a damp towel and heat in a 350°F oven for 10 to 15 minutes.

Green Leaf and Cilantro Salad

- 1 head each butter and red leaf lettuce, torn
  Half a jicama or daikon, coarsely shredded or sliced
- 1 bunch cilantro, stems removed
- ½ cup taco sauce or salsa
- ¼ cup salad oil
- 3 tablespoons vinegar

1. Mix lettuce, jicama, and cilantro.

2. Thoroughly combine remaining ingredients and pour over salad. Toss.

C O O K I N G   P L A N

1. Assemble all ingredients and cooking equipment.

2. Preheat oven to 350°F.

3. Chop all ingredients for turkey dish.

4. Cook turkey.

5. Warm pita bread in oven.

6. Prepare salad and dressing.

To serve: Dress salad. Remove pitas from oven and assemble turkey pitas.

Turkey Breast Cutlets

Parslied Parsnips

Steamed Kale and Pearl Onions

Poppy Seed Rolls

Wine suggestion:
Sylvaner Riesling

Turkey Breast Cutlets

Turkey has a mild flavor that lends itself to numerous taste combinations. Treated like veal, it offers an excellent substitute at an affordable price. You can also use pounded turkey tenderloin in this recipe.

> 1 to 1½ pounds turkey breast cutlets *or* 1 turkey breast (1½ to 2 lbs), sliced into cutlets
> 1 egg lightly beaten with ¼ cup milk
> 1 cup flour
> 2 tablespoons *each* butter and oil
> ¼ cup lemon juice
> ¼ cup butter
> Minced chives, for garnish

1. Pound cutlets between 2 sheets of plastic wrap (do not tear meat) to a thickness of ⅛ inch.

2. Dip cutlets in egg-milk mixture, then in flour. Shake off excess. To brown correctly, cutlets should be coated just before cooking.

3. Warm serving platter in 250°F oven.

4. Sauté cutlets in butter and oil over medium-high heat until golden (3 minutes per side). This can be done quickly in 2 large skillets. Transfer to warm platter.

5. Add lemon juice and butter to one of the skillets, bring to a boil, and reduce slightly. Pour sauce over cutlets and sprinkle with chives.

VARIATIONS

Sauté breaded or unbreaded cutlets as directed in Step 4, and select one of these sauces or toppings.

Cutlets Piccata

Add ¼ cup *each* lemon juice, butter, and chopped fresh parsley to skillet. Mix in 2 tablespoons capers, heat, and pour over cutlets.

Cutlets Saltimbocca

Top each cutlet with 1 slice prosciutto and 1 slice provolone cheese. Broil until cheese melts and turns golden.

Cutlets Marsala

Add ¼ cup butter, 2 or 3 minced cloves garlic, ⅓ cup Marsala wine, and ¼ cup *each* chopped fresh parsley and mushrooms to skillet. Heat; pour over cutlets.

Asparagus-and-Cheese Cutlets

Top each cutlet with 2 to 3 cooked asparagus spears and 2 tablespoons grated (or 1 slice) Swiss cheese. Broil until cheese melts and turns golden. Garnish with lemon wedges.

Mustard Cutlets

Pour ¼ cup white wine into skillet, bring to a boil, and reduce by half. Stir in ⅔ to 1 cup whipping cream and 3 to 4 tablespoons Dijon-style mustard. Reduce over high heat until thickened, and pour over cutlets.

Peppery Turkey Tarragon

Pour ½ cup white wine into skillet, bring to a boil, and reduce. Add 2 to 3 tablespoons chopped fresh tarragon leaves (or ½ teaspoon dried), 2 to 3 tablespoons drained green peppercorns, and ⅔ cup whipping cream. Reduce over high heat until thickened. Pour over cutlets.

Turkey with Mushrooms

Pour ½ cup sherry into skillet. Mix in 1 tablespoon butter, 2 to 3 tablespoons Dijon-style mustard, and 1½ to 2 cups sliced fresh mushrooms. Cook over high heat until mushrooms are tender and liquid is reduced by half. Stir in ⅔ to 1 cup whipping cream and reduce over high heat until thickened. Pour over cutlets.

Turkey Parmigiana

Place a layer of cutlets in a large baking dish, top with ½ cup *each* tomato sauce and shredded mozzarella *or* provolone cheese. Add remaining cutlets, overlapping slightly, and an additional ½ cup *each* tomato sauce and shredded cheese. Bake at 450°F until bubbly (5 to 10 minutes).

Turkey Sorrel (or Spinach)

In cutlet skillet, sauté 1 bunch chopped fresh sorrel *or* spinach leaves and ¼ cup chopped onion (optional) in 3 tablespoons butter until wilted (3 to 4 minutes). Remove. Add ¼ cup white wine; bring to a boil to reduce. Stir in 1 cup whipping cream and the sorrel. Serve over cutlets.

Try the Asparagus-and-Cheese variation of this basic, versatile recipe.

Pound turkey into tender cutlets, top with a tasty sauce, and see if family and guests aren't fooled by this low-cost substitute for veal.

Parslied Parsnips

1½ pounds (8 to 10) medium parsnips or carrots, peeled and trimmed
Boiling water
2 tablespoons butter
½ teaspoon dried basil
¼ cup minced fresh parsley

1. In a large, covered frying pan, cook parsnips in enough boiling water to cover until tender-crisp (about 15 minutes). Drain.

2. Add butter, basil, and parsley. Toss to coat parsnips.

Steamed Kale and Pearl Onions

¼ pound pearl onions, peeled, *or* white boiling onions, peeled and halved

1 bunch kale *or* chard, roughly chopped
Boiling water for steaming
Lemon wedges, for garnish

1. Place onions and then kale in steamer over boiling water and cook until kale is wilted (8 to 10 minutes).

2. Garnish with lemon wedges.

Poppy Seed Rolls

Warm 4 to 6 bakery rolls in a 250°F oven for 15 minutes.

C O O K I N G   P L A N

1. Assemble all ingredients and cooking equipment.

2. Pound cutlets.

3. Clean parsnips; chop basil and parsley. Clean kale, peel onions, and slice lemon.

4. Heat water for parsnips and for kale. Begin cooking parsnips.

5. Place egg-milk mixture and flour in 2 bowls and bread cutlets.

6. Put rolls and platter for turkey in 250°F oven.

7. Sauté cutlets and begin cooking kale.

8. Make sauce for cutlets.

9. Add flavorings to parsnips.

To serve: Remove rolls from oven. Pour sauce over cutlets; garnish. Serve kale and parsnips.

35

Apples, apple brandy, and cream make a rich, fruity sauce that also acts as a counterpoint to the vinaigrette that flavors the salad. The almonds add texture to this special meal.

20

Veal Normande

Rice with Almonds

Tomato-Cucumber Vinaigrette

Wine suggestion:
Gamay Beaujolais or Johannisberg Riesling

Veal Normande

This dish originated in France's Normandy province, where apples and dairy products are plentiful. The flavors are quite compatible. Boneless chicken breasts or turkey breast slices, pounded to a thickness of ⅛ inch, may be substituted for the veal.

- 1½ pounds boneless veal slices (¼ in. thick)
- ½ cup flour
- 1 tablespoon *each* butter and oil
- ¼ cup Calvados (apple brandy), brandy, *or* dry white wine
- 2 tart green apples, cored and thinly sliced
- ½ cup sour cream

1. Place veal between 2 pieces of plastic wrap and pound to a thickness of ⅛ inch. Coat with flour.

2. Warm serving platter in 200°F oven.

3. Melt butter and oil in a wide frying pan over medium-high heat.

4. Sauté veal until lightly browned but still pale pink inside (about 2 minutes per side). Remove to warm platter.

5. Add Calvados, scraping bottom of pan to free browned bits.

6. Add apple slices and sauté 3 to 5 minutes.

7. Reduce heat, stir in sour cream, and simmer until warm.

8. Top veal with a little of the sauce. Serve remaining sauce separately.

VARIATIONS

Sauté veal as directed through Step 4.

Veal Marsala

Add 2 tablespoons flour to skillet. Cook, stirring, until bubbly. Stir in ½ cup Marsala wine and cook until thickened. Pour sauce over veal and garnish with minced chives.

Veal Amandine

To sauté pan, add 1 tablespoon butter, 1 minced clove garlic, and ½ cup sliced almonds. Sauté until golden. Add ¼ cup Marsala, port, *or* dry sherry. Bring to a boil and ignite. For a creamy sauce, stir in ¼ cup sour *or* whipping cream. Pour sauce over veal and garnish with lemon wheels.

Rice with Almonds

- 2 cups water
- ½ teaspoon salt
- 1 cup white rice
- 1½ tablespoons butter
- 1 bag (2½ oz) sliced almonds

1. Bring water, salt, and rice to a boil. Cover, reduce heat, and simmer until all water is absorbed (20 minutes).

2. In a small skillet, melt butter. When it froths, add almonds and sauté until lightly browned.

3. Stir nuts into rice before serving.

Tomato-Cucumber Vinaigrette

For an attractive presentation, take a few minutes to arrange each salad individually. Slices of avocado, radish, turnip, or jicama (a Mexican root vegetable) make crispy additions. For fullest flavor, serve at room temperature.

- 1 bunch watercress
- 4 medium tomatoes, sliced
  Half a cucumber, peeled in alternate strips and thinly sliced
- 1 small red *or* yellow onion, thinly sliced and separated into rings

Vinaigrette:

- ¼ cup olive *or* other oil
- 2 tablespoons lemon juice
- 1 teaspoon Dijon-style mustard
- 1 teaspoon *each* minced fresh *or* ¼ teaspoon dried tarragon and thyme

1. Line plates or bowls with sprigs of watercress.

2. Alternate rings of tomato and cucumber. Top with onion rings. Garnish center with watercress sprigs.

3. Mix vinaigrette; pour over vegetables.

C O O K I N G   P L A N

1. Assemble all ingredients and cooking equipment.

2. Start rice.

3. Wash and slice vegetables for salad; assemble. Make vinaigrette; pour over vegetables.

4. Mince parsley and slice apples for veal; measure other ingredients.

5. Pound and coat veal.

6. Heat oven to 200°F and sauté veal.

7. While veal cooks, sauté almonds for rice.

8. Remove veal and prepare sauce.

To serve: Mix rice and almonds; serve salads. Top veal with a bit of the sauce, and serve remainder separately.

Veal Orloff

Minted Green Peas and Lettuce

Sourdough or Sweet French Rolls

Wine suggestion:
Brut or Extra Dry Champagne

Veal Orloff

A thick, rich sauce of cream, Champagne, and mushroom caps enhances this classic French dish. Use veal scallops or ask your butcher to cut a boneless veal roast into ¼-inch-thick slices across the grain.

- 1½ pounds boneless veal slices (¼ in. thick)
- ½ cup flour
- ¼ teaspoon salt
- ⅛ teaspoon pepper
- ⅛ teaspoon nutmeg
- 2 tablespoons *each* butter and oil
- ½ pound (20 medium) mushrooms, stems removed
- 2 shallots, chopped *or* 2 tablespoons minced onion
- ½ cup *each* whipping cream and sour cream
- ¼ cup Champagne *or* dry white wine Lemon wheels, for garnish

1. Place veal slices between 2 sheets of plastic wrap and pound to a thickness of ⅛ inch. Cut into strips across the grain.

2. Place flour, salt, pepper, and nutmeg in paper bag. Add veal and shake to coat.

3. Warm serving platter in 200°F oven.

4. Heat butter and oil in sauté pan over medium-high heat.

5. Sauté about half the veal, tossing occasionally, until strips turn a light golden brown (3 to 5 minutes). Remove to heated platter.

6. Sauté remaining veal strips. Remove to platter and keep warm in oven.

7. Add mushroom caps and shallots to pan and sauté briefly, scraping pan to release browned bits.

8. Return any veal juices from platter to pan. Add Champagne and whipping cream and reduce liquid by half over high heat.

9. Lower heat to simmer and stir in sour cream. Heat through.

10. To serve, spoon sauce over veal. Surround with lemon wheels.

Veal slices in a rich cream-and-Champagne sauce make an elegant and festive entrée. With a simple but colorful vegetable dish and bread, the meal is complete.

VARIATION

Veal Parmesan

Coat veal with ¼ cup *each* flour and freshly grated Parmesan cheese, ¼ teaspoon salt, ⅛ teaspoon pepper, and ¼ teaspoon paprika. Sauté in 1 tablespoon *each* butter and oil; remove to ovenproof serving dish. Top with ½ cup shredded mozzarella cheese and a dash of paprika. Broil until cheese is golden and bubbly (2 to 3 minutes). Sprinkle with chopped parsley and garnish with lemon wheels.

Minted Green Peas with Lettuce

- 2 tablespoons butter
- 10 ounces (half a 20-oz bag) frozen peas
- 2 cups (packed) shredded lettuce
- 1 tablespoon chopped fresh *or* 1 teaspoon dried mint leaves, crushed
- 2 tablespoons minced parsley (optional)
  Salt and sugar (optional) to taste

1. Melt butter in a large frying pan over medium heat. Add peas (breaking up with a fork), cover, and cook until thawed (about 5 minutes).

2. Add lettuce, mint, and parsley and cook, uncovered, until lettuce wilts. Toss occasionally. Season.

Sourdough or Sweet French Rolls

Warm 4 to 6 purchased rolls in a 200°F oven for 15 minutes.

COOKING PLAN

1. Assemble all ingredients and cooking equipment.

2. Remove peas from package to thaw slightly.

3. Prepare mushrooms, chop shallots, and slice lemon for veal.

4. Shred lettuce and mince parsley for peas.

5. Place rolls and platter in 200°F oven.

6. Pound, slice, and coat veal. Sauté.

7. Begin cooking peas.

8. Remove veal from pan and prepare sauce.

9. While sauce cooks, add lettuce to peas.

To serve: Remove rolls from oven. Pour sauce over veal and garnish. Season peas and serve.

Beef Filet with Béarnaise and Tomato

Fruited Savoy Cabbage

Baguette

Wine suggestion:
French Côtes-du-Rhône

Filets, as well as most quality cuts of beef, are enhanced by Béarnaise sauce. Since this golden sauce is also wonderful poured over vegetables and eggs and is a snap to prepare in the blender, why not make it a staple in your cooking repertoire? The honeyed flavor of the crispy cabbage-apple duo in this menu is a tasty counterpoint to the Béarnaise.

Beef Filet with Béarnaise and Tomato

Filet mignon is the cut traditionally used in this recipe, but less expensive cuts such as flank, top round, and chuck can be substituted. Reduce cooking time on these cuts to 4 to 6 minutes per side for rare meat. Test doneness by the amount of resistance the steak has to pressure. The firmer the steak, the more well done it is.

The 30-minute cooking plan assumes the steaks will be cooked indoors in the broiler. If you choose to grill the steaks outdoors over coals, allow additional time to ready the coals for cooking.

- 4 filet mignon steaks, 1½ to 2 inches thick
- 2 large tomatoes
  Blender Béarnaise (recipe follows)

1. Preheat broiler.

2. Slice tomatoes and set aside.

3. About 20 minutes before serving, place steaks in broiler 4 inches from heat source. Broil 7 or 8 minutes per side for rare meat.

4. To serve, top each steak with 1 or 2 slices of tomato and cover with Blender Béarnaise.

Blender Béarnaise

- ¼ cup *each* wine vinegar and vermouth *or* white wine
- 1 teaspoon dried tarragon
- ¼ cup minced green onion (optional)
- 1 cup (2 cubes) butter
- 3 egg yolks

1. In a small saucepan, bring vinegar, vermouth, tarragon, and onion to a boil. Reduce to 3 tablespoons.

2. Melt butter in separate saucepan.

3. In blender, whirl yolks just until blended. Add reduced wine mixture and blend briefly.

4. Add butter, at first a droplet at a time, blending continuously on high speed. As mixture thickens, increase butter to a thin stream.

5. Keep sauce warm by placing blender container in a pan of lukewarm water if desired.

Note: If sauce "breaks," or curdles, beat in 1 tablespoon water.

Fruited Savoy Cabbage

- 2 tablespoons butter
- 1 medium-size Savoy cabbage, trimmed and cut crosswise into ½-inch strips
- 1 cup thinly sliced green apple *or* ½ cup coarsely chopped canned water chestnuts
- 2 tablespoons honey
- 1 teaspoon salt

1. Melt butter in a large skillet over medium-high heat. Add cabbage and sauté, tossing often, for 4 minutes.

2. Stir in apple, honey, and salt. Sauté, tossing occasionally, until tender-crisp (4 to 6 minutes).

Baguette

Warm purchased baguette briefly in oven after removing steak from broiler, or serve at room temperature.

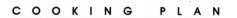

COOKING PLAN

1. Assemble all ingredients and cooking equipment.

2. Preheat broiler.

3. Wash and slice cabbage, apples, and tomatoes.

4. Place steaks in broiler.

5. Prepare Béarnaise.

6. Sauté cabbage.

7. Turn steaks.

8. Add apples to cabbage.

9. Remove steaks; turn off broiler and place bread in oven to warm.

To serve: Garnish steaks with tomato and Béarnaise. Accompany with cabbage and bread.

Steak with Green Peppercorns

White Rice

Fresh Buttered Asparagus

Wine suggestion:
Australian Cabernet Shiraz
or Cabernet Sauvignon

This rich and fiery sauce is as delicious as it looks. For an esoteric alternative, use pink peppercorns. Or substitute cracked black peppercorns.

Steak with Green Peppercorns

- 1 teaspoon *each* butter and oil
- 1 top round, sirloin, *or* flank steak (1½ lbs)
- ¼ cup brandy
- ½ cup minced green or red onion *or* ¼ cup shallots
- 2 to 3 tablespoons green peppercorns, rinsed
- ⅓ cup *each* dry white wine and whipping cream
- 1 tablespoon Dijon-style mustard
- 1 tablespoon chopped fresh *or* ½ teaspoon dried tarragon
  Salt and freshly ground pepper to taste
  Watercress leaves, for garnish

1. Heat butter and oil in a wide frying pan over medium-high heat. Brown steak well on both sides (3 to 5 minutes per side for rare meat).

2. Add brandy to pan, heat, and ignite, shaking until flames die. Remove meat to a carving board.

3. Add remaining ingredients (except watercress) to pan, increase heat to high, and reduce sauce until shiny bubbles form.

4. While sauce cooks, slice meat diagonally (across the grain for flank steak).

5. To serve, top steak with sauce and garnish with watercress.

VARIATIONS

For all variations, cook steak as directed in Step 1. Remove to carving board.

Steak with Mushroom-and-Wine Sauce

In frying pan, sauté ¼ pound sliced mushrooms and 2 minced cloves garlic in 1 tablespoon butter. Combine ⅓ cup *each* red wine or port and beef broth with a mixture of 1 tablespoon cornstarch, 1 teaspoon Dijon-style mustard, ½ teaspoon anchovy paste (optional), and 2 tablespoons minced parsley *or* green onion. Add to pan, bring sauce to a boil, reduce heat, and simmer until thickened. Pour over sliced steak.

Carbonnade du Nord

In frying pan, sauté 1 thinly sliced sweet red onion in 1 tablespoon butter. Add 1 tablespoon flour and ½ cup dark beer. Bring to a boil, reduce heat, and simmer until thickened. Pour over sliced steak.

Steak Provençal

In frying pan, sauté 1 sliced red *or* green pepper, 1 thinly sliced small red onion, 1 large tomato (cut in 8 wedges), and 2 minced cloves garlic in 1 tablespoon olive oil. Add ¼ cup beef broth, ½ teaspoon dried oregano, ⅛ teaspoon rosemary, and 1 tablespoon chopped fresh basil *or* parsley. Stir to combine and pour over sliced steak.

White Rice

- 2 cups water
- ½ teaspoon salt
- 1 cup white rice

Bring ingredients to a boil. Cover, reduce heat, and simmer until all water is absorbed (20 minutes).

Fresh Buttered Asparagus

- 1½ to 2 pounds asparagus
  Boiling salted water
- 2 tablespoons butter

1. Wash asparagus and cut or snap off tough ends.

2. In a wide frying pan in a little boiling water, lay spears parallel, no more than 3 layers deep. Cook, uncovered, over high heat until stems are just tender when pierced with a fork (6 to 8 minutes).

3. Drain and top with butter.

VARIATIONS

For a flavorful change, melt the butter and add ⅛ teaspoon nutmeg and the juice of half a lemon to it. Or, substitute 1 tablespoon soy sauce, 2 tablespoons sesame seed, and 2 teaspoons freshly grated ginger for the butter.

C O O K I N G   P L A N

1. Assemble all ingredients and cooking equipment.

2. Start rice.

3. Chop onion and wash watercress for steak. Clean asparagus.

4. Brown steak.

5. Heat water for asparagus. Begin to cook it when you turn the steak.

6. Add brandy to steak.

7. Make sauce for steak and slice meat.

8. Melt butter for asparagus.

To serve: Fluff rice. Spoon sauce over meat and garnish. Butter asparagus.

Steak Bonne Femme

Steamed New Potatoes

Glazed Sesame-Seed Carrots

Wine suggestion:
Nonvintage Bordeaux or Burgundy

Steak Bonne Femme

  1 tablespoon *each* butter and oil
  1 large red onion, thinly sliced and separated into rings
  ½ pound (20 medium) mushrooms, sliced
  1 clove garlic, minced
1½ pounds top sirloin steak (¾ in. thick), cut into 4 equal pieces
  ¼ cup beef broth *or* dry vermouth
    Salt and freshly ground pepper to taste

1. Warm serving platter in 200°F oven.

2. Heat butter and oil in a large frying pan over medium heat. Add onion, mushrooms, and garlic and sauté until softened.

3. Increase heat to brown onion and reduce mushroom juices. Remove vegetables from pan.

4. In same pan over high heat, adding a little more butter and oil if necessary, brown steaks until done to taste (3 to 4 minutes per side for rare). Remove to heated platter.

5. Add broth to pan; bring to a boil to reduce liquid, scraping pan to loosen browned bits.

6. Reduce heat, stir in reserved onion-mushroom-garlic mixture, and heat through. Spoon sauce over steaks.

Steamed New Potatoes

10 to 12 small new red *or* white potatoes
    Boiling water
    Minced parsley

1. Scrub potatoes, but do not peel. Slice thinly.

2. Place in basket or perforated container over boiling water. Place carrots on top. (See recipe for Glazed Sesame-Seed Carrots.)

3. Steam 15 minutes or until tender.

4. Remove from steamer and sprinkle with parsley.

Glazed Sesame-Seed Carrots

  8 to 10 medium carrots, peeled and cut in 3-inch sticks
  2 tablespoons sesame seed
  1 teaspoon butter
  2 tablespoons butter
  1 tablespoon honey
  1 tablespoon grated orange peel
  1 teaspoon grated ginger root (optional)

1. Place carrots in steamer above potatoes. (See recipe for Steamed New Potatoes.) Cook 15 minutes or until tender.

2. While carrots steam, toast sesame seed in the 1 teaspoon butter in a medium-size skillet until golden.

3. When carrots are tender, add the 2 tablespoons butter, honey, and orange peel to the sesame seed. Remove carrots from steamer and toss in glaze.

C O O K I N G   P L A N

1. Assemble all ingredients and cooking equipment.

2. Heat water in steamer.

3. Wash and slice potatoes and carrots.

4. Slice onion and mushrooms; mince garlic and parsley; grate orange peel.

5. Place potatoes and carrots in steamer, with potatoes on bottom.

6. Warm platter in 200°F oven.

7. Sauté vegetables for steaks.

8. Toast sesame seed.

9. Sauté steaks.

10. Glaze carrots.

To serve: Sprinkle potatoes with parsley. Spoon sauce over steak and serve carrots.

Onions and mushrooms characterize this tasty sirloin steak sauce. Served attractively on a platter with orange-flavored sesame-seed carrots and steamed new potatoes, this traditional entrée becomes truly special.

Classic Hamburgers with International Toppings

Red-and-Green Cabbage Salad

Beverage suggestion:
A light beer

Classic Hamburgers with International Toppings

For the most flavorful and juicy burgers, buy coarsely ground meat with 20% fat. Use approximately 5 ounces of meat for each patty. Line your broiler with aluminum foil to simplify cleanup.

The main recipe features a cooked-with-the-burger topping, but you may substitute any of the variations, which should be added to plain broiled burgers immediately before serving. For a cookout or special occasion, make a selection of toppings and offer family and guests a choice.

Sourdough French rolls, whole wheat pita bread, or cheese English muffins are alternatives to plain English muffins or the traditional hamburger bun.

1¼ pounds ground chuck or beef (20% fat)
1 sweet red onion, thinly sliced
1 large green pepper, seeded and cut into ¼-inch-thick rings
2 teaspoons crushed dried oregano mixed with 1 to 2 tablespoons olive oil
4 English muffins, split

1. Preheat broiler.

2. Shape ground meat into 4 patties.

3. Lightly grease broiler rack and broil first side of burgers 4 inches from heat source until desired doneness is reached. Broiling time *per side* is:

Rare	4 minutes
Medium	6 minutes
Well done	7 to 8 minutes

4. Turn burgers, top each with 1 slice onion, 1 green pepper ring, and ¼ of the oregano-oil mixture.

5. During last 3 minutes of cooking time, place muffins, cut side up, on rack with burgers to brown.

INTERNATIONAL TOPPINGS

Broil burgers on both sides as directed above, but do not top with onion, pepper, oregano, and oil. Select a topping and fit it into the Cooking Plan.

Guacamole Burgers

Combine 1 small mashed avocado (1 cup), 1 small chopped tomato *or* ¼ cup Mexican salsa, 1 tablespoon lemon juice, ½ teaspoon chili powder, and salt and pepper to taste. Place a spoonful on each broiled burger and top with sliced olives and chopped tomato. For variety, serve burgers on fried corn tortillas instead of buns.

French Tarragon Butter Burgers

In a small saucepan, combine ½ to 1 teaspoon dried tarragon with 1 tablespoon white wine vinegar. Boil until liquid is almost gone. When cooled slightly, mix tarragon and 3 tablespoons minced parsley into ¼ cup softened butter. Top each broiled burger with ¼ of the seasoned butter.

Health Salad Burgers

Combine 1 shredded medium carrot, ¼ cup sour cream *or* yogurt, and 2 tablespoons wheat germ. Place a spoonful on each broiled burger and top each with 1 teaspoon sunflower seed.

Russian Burgers

On each broiled burger, place 1 tablespoon sour cream *or* yogurt. Top with 2 teaspoons red, black, *or* golden caviar. Garnish each with ¼ of a finely chopped green onion.

Mushroom-and-Wine Sauced Burgers

Sauté ¼ pound sliced mushrooms and 2 minced cloves garlic in 1 tablespoon butter. Combine ⅓ cup *each* dry red wine *or* port and beef broth with a mixture of 1 tablespoon cornstarch, 1 teaspoon Dijon-style mustard, ½ teaspoon anchovy paste (optional), and 2 tablespoons minced parsley *or* green onion. Add to mushrooms, bring to a boil, reduce heat, and simmer until thickened. Spoon over broiled burgers.

Burgers Provencal

Sauté 1 sliced red *or* green pepper, 1 chopped medium red *or* yellow onion, and 2 minced cloves garlic in 1 tablespoon olive oil. Sprinkle with ½ teaspoon dried oregano, ⅛ teaspoon rosemary, and 1 tablespoon chopped fresh basil *or* parsley. Stir to combine and spoon over broiled burgers.

Burgers Rancheros

Substitute sliced French bread for the muffins. Top each slice with 2 slices of cheese and broil 1 minute. Add a slice of tomato, a broiled burger, a fried *or* poached egg, and sliced ripe olives *or* chopped chives for garnish.

Anchovy Burgers

Substitute sourdough French rolls for the muffins. Top each roll with 2 slices Swiss *or* Monterey jack cheese and broil until cheese melts. Add to each roll ¼ cup sautéed sliced red onions (optional) and a burger. Top with anchovy fillets and pimiento slices crisscrossed in a checkerboard pattern. Place halved green olives in the "squares."

Red-and-Green Cabbage Salad

½ head green cabbage, sliced or shredded
½ large red onion, thinly sliced *or* chopped
½ to ⅔ cup mayonnaise
Juice of half a lemon
¼ teaspoon lemon pepper *or* black pepper

Mix all ingredients and chill.

C O O K I N G   P L A N

1. Assemble all ingredients and cooking equipment.

2. Choose your topping and fit it into the Cooking Plan.

3. Wash and slice vegetables for salad. Prepare and refrigerate.

4. Preheat broiler.

5. Shape burgers and broil. Allow a total time of 8 minutes (for rare) to 16 minutes (for well done).

6. Turn burgers.

7. Place muffins under broiler.

To serve: Remove salad from refrigerator. Place each burger on a muffin. Spoon on topping if necessary.

An old-time favorite with an international twist. Barbeque or broil the patties, but serve them with one or a choice of several toppings. The Red-and-Green Cabbage Salad in this menu is a great picnic item, or choose any salad that suits your mood or menu.

Curried Chicken Livers

Elbow Macaroni

Butter-Steamed Chard
with Lemon Mayonnaise

Beverage suggestion:
A full-bodied beer or ale

Curried Chicken Livers

- 1 pound chicken livers
- 1 tablespoon *each* butter and oil
- 1 tablespoon dry mustard
- 2 to 3 teaspoons curry powder
- 1 tablespoon ground ginger
- 1 clove garlic, minced
- 1 cup frozen peas
- 3 tablespoons chopped green onion

1. Rinse and drain livers; pat dry. Cut livers in half.

2. Heat butter and oil over medium-high heat in a heavy skillet. Add mustard, curry powder, ginger, and garlic and sauté 10 seconds.

3. Add livers and sauté until browned (8 to 10 minutes).

4. Add peas and cook, covered, until tender (about 5 minutes).

5. Sprinkle with green onion before serving.

VARIATIONS

Livers with Madeira Wine Sauce

Sauté ⅔ cup sliced fresh mushrooms in 2 tablespoons butter. Add 1 cup chicken broth and ⅓ cup Madeira. Stir in 2 teaspoons tomato paste. In a small bowl, blend 1 teaspoon cornstarch with 1 tablespoon cold water. Stir into sauce and simmer 10 minutes. While sauce simmers, sauté livers in 1 tablespoon *each* butter and oil. Pour sauce over livers.

Livers with Creole Sauce

Heat 2 tablespoons olive oil in a saucepan. Add ½ cup *each* chopped red onion and celery. Cook, stirring, until onion becomes limp. Add 2 cups chopped fresh *or* canned plum tomatoes, 1 bay leaf, ½ teaspoon dried rosemary, and ¼ to ½ teaspoon dried red pepper flakes. Bring to a boil, reduce heat, and simmer 10 minutes. While sauce simmers, sauté livers in 1 tablespoon *each* butter and oil. Pour sauce over livers.

If you like liver, you'll love the sauce variations with this menu. The Lemon Mayonnaise dressing for the butter-steamed chard can also top broccoli or asparagus.

Elbow Macaroni

- 2 quarts water
- 1 teaspoon salt
- 8 ounces elbow macaroni (green and yellow vegetable pasta preferred, for color)
- 2 tablespoons olive oil
- 1 teaspoon lemon juice

1. Bring salted water to a boil.

2. Add macaroni, oil, and lemon juice and cook until tender but firm (6 to 9 minutes). Drain.

Butter-Steamed Chard with Lemon Mayonnaise

- 1¼ to 1½ pounds fresh chard
- 2 tablespoons butter
- 2 tablespoons water
- Lemon Mayonnaise (recipe follows)

1. Wash chard. Slice stems diagonally and chop leaves roughly.

2. Melt butter in a large, heavy skillet. Add chard stems; cover and cook 3 to 4 minutes.

3. Add leaves and sprinkle with water. Cover and cook 3 to 4 minutes longer or until tender.

4. Serve with Lemon Mayonnaise.

Lemon Mayonnaise

- ⅔ cup mayonnaise (at room temperature)
- Juice of 1 lemon
- 1 teaspoon Worcestershire sauce
- Salt and freshly ground pepper

Combine all ingredients; taste, and adjust seasonings if necessary.

COOKING PLAN

1. Assemble all ingredients and cooking equipment.

2. Measure mayonnaise. Wash and chop chard

3. Halve livers; chop and measure other ingredients.

4. Start water for macaroni.

5. Sauté livers.

6. Add macaroni to boiling water.

7. Butter-steam chard stems.

8. Prepare lemon mayonnaise.

9. Add peas to livers.

10. Add chard leaves to stems.

To serve: Drain macaroni, garnish liver, and top chard with lemon mayonnaise.

There are few, if any, fence sitters on the subject of liver. Properly sautéed and topped with mushrooms and onions, calves' liver is tender, nutritious, and delicious. Chunky vegetables and baked potato slices complete this hearty meal.

29

Hearty Calves' Liver

Baked Potato Slices

Zucchini-Tomato Provençal

Wine suggestion:
Zinfandel

Hearty Calves' Liver

1 pound thinly sliced calves' liver
½ cup flour seasoned with ½ teaspoon salt and ⅛ teaspoon pepper
2 tablespoons butter
½ cup *each* sliced onions and fresh mushrooms
¼ cup butter
Minced chives, for garnish

1. Coat liver with seasoned flour.

2. Melt the 2 tablespoons butter in a large, heavy skillet and sauté onions and mushrooms until tender. Remove from skillet.

3. Add the ¼ cup butter to the skillet and heat until it foams. Without crowding, sauté liver 2 minutes per side over medium-high heat. Do *not* overcook.

4. Top with onions and mushrooms and sprinkle with chives.

VARIATIONS

Liver Americana

Grill or fry 4 to 8 slices of bacon. Sauté ½ cup onions in 2 tablespoons butter. Top sautéed liver with onions and bacon.

Brandied Liver

Sauté ½ cup sliced fresh mushrooms in 2 tablespoons butter. Add 2 to 3 tablespoons brandy and spoon over sautéed liver.

Herbed Liver

In a saucepan, bring to a simmer ¼ cup butter, 2 to 3 tablespoons chopped green onion, 1 tablespoon red wine vinegar, 2 tablespoons minced parsley *or* chives, and ½ teaspoon tarragon leaves. Pour over sautéed liver.

Baked Potato Slices

4 large potatoes
Salt and freshly ground pepper
Chopped parsley and butter (optional), for garnish

1. Preheat oven to 400°F.

2. Scrub potatoes and cut crosswise into ⅛-inch-thick slices. Season to taste.

3. Bake on oiled cookie sheet until tender (about 20 minutes). Check after 10 minutes and turn slices as they brown.

4. Garnish with parsley and butter if desired.

Zucchini-Tomato Provençal

2 firm zucchini (about 1 lb)
2 tablespoons olive oil
1 to 2 large cloves garlic, minced
12 cherry tomatoes
½ teaspoon dried basil *or* oregano
Salt and freshly ground pepper

1. Trim ends from zucchini and quarter lengthwise. Holding quarters together, cut crosswise into ½-inch-thick slices.

2. Heat oil in a large skillet over medium-high heat and sauté zucchini and garlic until zucchini starts to brown (5 minutes).

3. Add tomatoes and basil and continue to sauté until tomatoes are warm (2 to 4 minutes). Season to taste.

C O O K I N G   P L A N

1. Assemble all ingredients and cooking equipment.

2. Preheat oven to 400°F. Prepare potatoes and place in oven.

3. Slice mushrooms, onions, and zucchini. Mince chives, parsley, and garlic.

4. Check potatoes and turn if brown. Dredge liver.

5. Sauté mushrooms and onions for liver. Begin zucchini sauté.

6. Check potatoes; turn off oven if done.

7. Sauté liver. Add tomatoes to zucchini.

To serve: Remove potatoes from oven and garnish. Top liver with sauce and serve zucchini.

Bulgar Pilaf

Chopped green pepper, slivered almonds, grated carrot, and sliced ripe olives make tasty and colorful additions to the basic pilaf.

- 2 tablespoons butter
- 1 to 3 cloves garlic, minced
- ¼ cup *each* chopped yellow *or* green onion, mushrooms, and celery
- 1 cup bulgar
- 2 cups chicken broth
- 2 to 3 tablespoons minced fresh parsley
- 2 tablespoons chopped pimiento (optional)
  Salt and freshly ground pepper to taste

1. Melt butter in large skillet over medium-high heat. Add garlic, vegetables, and bulgar and sauté, stirring occasionally, until bulgar is golden.

2. Add broth, bring to a boil, reduce heat, and simmer, covered, 15 minutes.

3. Just before serving, stir in parsley, pimiento, and salt and pepper.

Golden Cauliflower

- 3 tablespoons butter
- 4 cups thinly sliced cauliflower
- ⅓ cup water
- 1 cup shredded Cheddar cheese
- 1 teaspoon paprika

1. Melt butter in large skillet. Add cauliflower and water. Cover and steam over high heat for 3 minutes.

2. Top with cheese and paprika; cover and continue steaming until cheese melts and cauliflower is tender (about 2 minutes).

Loin chops as thick as steaks are easily barbequed. Serve them straight off the grill or try the savory mustard sauce as a counterpoint to the cheesy cauliflower.

30

Savory Broiled Pork Chops

Bulgar Pilaf

Golden Cauliflower

Wine suggestion:
Pinot Noir

Savory Broiled Pork Chops

- 4 pork loin chops, *each* ¾ inch thick
- 3 tablespoons Dijon-style mustard
- 1 teaspoon dried thyme, crushed
  Salt and freshly ground pepper to taste

1. Preheat broiler.

2. Spread half the mustard evenly over chops; sprinkle with half the thyme.

3. Broil 6 inches from heat source 10 to 12 minutes. Turn chops, spread with remaining mustard, and sprinkle with thyme and salt and pepper.

4. Broil second side until nicely browned (10 to 12 minutes). Juices should run clear when chop is pierced with a fork at thickest point.

VARIATION

Pork Chops with Cumberland Sauce

In a small saucepan, combine ½ cup red currant jelly, ⅓ cup *each* orange juice and port, grated peel of 1 orange, and 2 tablespoons lemon juice mixed with 1 teaspoon dry mustard and ½ teaspoon ground ginger. Heat, stirring, until jelly melts. Spoon a little of the sauce over plain broiled chops; serve remainder separately. This sauce is excellent with any full-flavored meat or game.

C O O K I N G   P L A N

1. Assemble all ingredients and cooking equipment.

2. Preheat broiler.

3. Spread chops with mustard, add thyme, and place in broiler.

4. Chop vegetables for pilaf and sauté with bulgar. Add broth and simmer.

5. Wash and slice cauliflower; shred cheese.

6. Check chops and turn if ready.

7. Cook cauliflower; a few minutes later, add cheese and paprika.

8. Test chops by piercing with a fork.

To serve: Add parsley, pimiento, and seasonings to pilaf. Remove chops from broiler. Serve cauliflower.

Apricot Pork Chops

Poppy Seed Egg Noodles

Sautéed Cabbage and Peas

Wine suggestion:
Red Rioja or Chianti Classico

Apricot Pork Chops

- 1 tablespoon butter
- 4 thinly sliced loin pork chops
- 1 cup sliced red *or* yellow onion
- 1 cup beef broth
- ½ cup port *or* red or white wine (or increase broth to 1½ cups)
- ½ cup dried apricot halves
- ¼ cup orange marmalade
- 1 teaspoon grated fresh ginger root *or* ½ teaspoon ground ginger
  Dash *each* nutmeg and garlic powder
- 1 tablespoon cornstarch
  Lemon wedges, for garnish

1. In a large skillet over medium-high heat, melt butter and brown chops 2 to 3 minutes per side.

2. Combine remaining ingredients (except cornstarch and lemon wedges) and pour over meat.

3. Bring to a boil, reduce heat, cover, and simmer until meat is tender (15 to 20 minutes).

4. Mix cornstarch with a tablespoon of the sauce and then add to skillet. Cook, stirring, until sauce thickens.

5. Garnish with lemon wedges.

VARIATIONS

Peachy Pork Chops

Brown chops and remove from skillet. Add ¼ cup *each* chopped onion and green pepper and sauté until tender. Return meat to pan and add 1 cup beef *or* chicken broth, 1½ teaspoons dried thyme, 1 teaspoon dry mustard, and ⅛ to ¼ teaspoon garlic powder. Cover and simmer 15 minutes. Add 2 halved fresh peaches *or* 1 can (16 oz) drained peach halves and 4 green pepper rings; simmer 5 minutes more. To serve, top each chop with sauce, a heated peach half, and a pepper ring.

Sweet-and-Sour Pork Chops

Brown chops as directed. Add ¾ cup beef *or* chicken broth and 1 tablespoon *each* soy sauce, brown sugar, and vinegar and simmer 10 minutes. Add half

Fresh or canned apricots may be substituted for dried, or use peaches or prunes. Cabbage and poppy seed offer a textural contrast to the fruited chops.

a sliced green pepper, 4 quartered small white onions, and 1 can (8 oz) pineapple chunks, drained. Cook, covered, until vegetables are tender (10 minutes). Mix 1 tablespoon cornstarch with a little of the sauce and then add to skillet. Cook, stirring, until sauce thickens.

Poppy Seed Egg Noodles

- 2 quarts water
- 1 teaspoon salt
- 8 ounces thin *or* medium egg noodles
- 3 tablespoons butter, whipping cream, *or* sour cream
- 2 tablespoons poppy seed

1. Bring salted water to a boil.

2. Add noodles and cook, uncovered, until tender but firm (4 to 8 minutes, depending on size). Drain.

3. Warm butter, whipping cream, or sour cream in pot in which noodles were cooked. Add noodles and poppy seed and toss gently to mix.

Sautéed Cabbage and Peas

- 2 tablespoons butter
- ½ small head cabbage, finely sliced, shredded, *or* processed (2½ cups)
- 10 ounces (half a 20-oz bag) frozen petite peas
  Nutmeg and white pepper to taste

1. Melt butter in large skillet and sauté cabbage until slightly wilted (3 minutes).

2. Add peas and seasonings and cook, stirring, until heated through (3 to 5 minutes).

C O O K I N G   P L A N

1. Assemble all ingredients and cooking equipment.

2. Brown chops.

3. Meanwhile, slice onion and lemon wedges for chops.

4. Add remaining ingredients to chops and simmer.

5. Heat water for noodles.

6. Wash and shred cabbage.

7. Add noodles to boiling water.

8. Sauté cabbage. Then, add peas.

9. Drain noodles and warm butter or cream.

To serve: Toss noodles with poppy seed and butter or cream. Garnish chops and serve cabbage.

Grilled Ham with Hot Peaches

Crunchy Health Slaw

Whole Wheat Rolls

Wine suggestion:
Grey Riesling or Rosé

Grilled Ham with Hot Peaches

  1 egg
  ½ cup milk
  1 pound deli ham, sliced ¼ inch thick
  ¾ to 1 cup bread crumbs
  2 tablespoons *each* butter and oil
  4 fresh peaches, sliced *or* 1 can
     (16 oz) Cling peach slices, drained
  ¼ cup honey

1. Preheat oven to 450°F.

2. Beat together egg and milk. Coat each ham slice first with egg mixture and then with bread crumbs.

3. In a large skillet heat butter and oil and brown slices on both sides.

4. Form slices into rolls and arrange in a row in a baking dish.

5. Place peach slices over ham and drizzle with honey. Bake until honey glazes (5 minutes).

⌐ VARIATIONS

Do not bread ham. Spread slices with one of the following glazes (do not roll) and broil glazed side 5 to 6 inches from heat source until slices are heated through (3 to 4 minutes).

Spicy Glazed Ham

Combine ¼ cup *each* honey and soy sauce and 1 teaspoon Dijon-style *or* regular mustard. Spread over slices.

Ham with Lime-Mustard Glaze

Mix ¼ cup dry mustard with ⅛ teaspoon salt. Add 1 to 2 tablespoons *each* cold water, white vinegar, and lime juice. If glaze is too nippy, add a little olive oil and a pinch of sugar. Spread over slices.

Ham with Tarragon-Mustard Glaze

Mix ¼ cup dry mustard with ⅛ teaspoon salt. Add 1 to 2 tablespoons *each* cold water and tarragon wine vinegar, and ½ teaspoon dried tarragon. If glaze is too nippy, add a little olive oil and a pinch of sugar. Spread over slices.

When fresh green or red pears are in season, they make a tasty and unusual substitute for the peaches. Be sure to try the variations for other delicious ham dinners.

Cranberry or Chutney-Glazed Ham

Spread about ⅓ cup cranberry relish *or* chutney over slices.

Crunchy Health Slaw

  1 medium head (2½ lbs) green
     cabbage, with outer leaves
  ¼ cup *each* plain yogurt and
     mayonnaise
  1 to 2 teaspoons honey
  ½ cup seedless red *or* green grapes
  1 tablespoon lemon juice
  4 tablespoons sunflower seed *or*
     slivered almonds
  2 to 3 tablespoons wheat germ
  ¼ teaspoon *each* celery seed and salt
  ⅛ teaspoon freshly ground black *or*
     white pepper
     Sunflower seed *or* slivered almonds,
     for garnish (optional)

1. Wash cabbage and turn back several rows of outer leaves. With a paring knife, cut stem at base of leaves to release center of cabbage, leaving outer leaves attached to stem to form a bowl. Drain outer leaves well.

2. Shred center of cabbage, place in mixing bowl, and fold in remaining ingredients. Chill.

3. Serve slaw in cabbage bowl. Sprinkle with additional sunflower seed *or* almonds if desired.

Whole Wheat Rolls

Wrap 4 to 6 purchased rolls in aluminum foil and warm in 450°F oven with ham slices for about 5 minutes.

C O O K I N G   P L A N

1. Assemble all ingredients and cooking equipment.

2. Preheat oven to 450°F.

3. Wash cabbage, cut apart to form bowl, and shred center. Wash grapes. Slice peaches for ham.

4. Combine ingredients for slaw and refrigerate.

5. Bread ham slices and brown.

6. Assemble ham dish. Place in oven along with rolls.

7. Spoon slaw into cabbage bowl.

To serve: Garnish slaw. Remove rolls and ham from oven and serve.

This colorful presentation makes a simple sausage more appealing. Serve with a spicy German or Dijon-style mustard, rounds of pumpernickel, and crisp kosher dill pickle spears. The apples add a sweet twist to the cabbage, topping off this German dinner.

33

Bratwurst

Spaetzle

Red Cabbage with Apples

Beverage suggestion:
German beer

Bratwurst

  4 bratwurst *or* knockwurst
     Boiling water
  1 cup sliced red *or* yellow onion
  1 tablespoon oil
  ½ cup grated Swiss cheese, at room
     temperature
  4 green pepper rings, for garnish

1. Simmer sausages in enough boiling water to cover for 10 minutes. Drain.

2. Meanwhile, in a large skillet sauté onion in oil until golden brown and limp (5 to 7 minutes). Remove from skillet and keep warm. Sauté drained sausages until golden. Add onions and warm briefly.

3. To serve, slice sausages lengthwise almost, but not quite, through skin. Place, cut side down, on a bed of sautéed onion; top with cheese and garnish with green pepper.

Spaetzle

Packaged dried spaetzle — noodle-like German egg dumplings — can be found in the imported food section of many supermarkets, or at delicatessens or specialty food shops. If they aren't available, substitute curly egg noodles.

Follow directions on a 10-ounce package of spaetzle. Cook in boiling, salted water (or beef or chicken broth, for more flavor) for 10 minutes. Then remove from heat and let stand in cooking water 10 minutes more. Drain and toss with butter. It's traditional to sprinkle spaetzle with bread crumbs before serving.

Red Cabbage with Apples

  1 onion, coarsely chopped
  2 tablespoons salad oil
  ¼ cup cider vinegar
  2 tablespoons brown sugar *or* honey
     Salt and pepper to taste
  1 green apple, cored and thinly sliced
  1 small head red cabbage, coarsely
     shredded

1. In a large skillet, sauté onion in oil until softened (5 minutes). Add vinegar, sugar, salt, and pepper; stir to mix.

2. Add apple and cabbage. Bring liquid to a boil, reduce heat to medium, cover, and cook until cabbage wilts (10 minutes). Stir occasionally to coat cabbage with vinegar-sugar mixture.

COOKING PLAN

1. Assemble all ingredients and cooking equipment.

2. Heat water for bratwurst and for spaetzle.

3. Chop apple, cabbage, and onion for red cabbage dish. Slice onion and green pepper and grate cheese for bratwurst.

4. Simmer sausages.

5. Add spaetzle to boiling water.

6. Sauté onion for bratwurst. Separately, sauté onion for cabbage dish.

7. Add liquid, and then apple and cabbage, to cabbage dish.

8. Remove spaetzle from heat and let stand.

9. Brown sausages and warm onions.

To serve: Slice bratwurst and arrange on onions; garnish. Drain spaetzle, toss with butter, and garnish. Serve cabbage.

34

Kielbasa One-Pot Supper

Spinach Salad
with Lemon-Soy Dressing

Dark Rye with Melted Cheese

Beverage suggestion:
A full-bodied beer or ale

What could be easier than a one-pot supper made with a precooked sausage? Lemon-soy dressing complements the fruited spinach salad, and the dark-rye melt-overs make this hearty dinner perfect for a fireside meal on a cold winter night.

Kielbasa One-Pot Supper

4 to 6 slices bacon, diced
1 tablespoon butter
4 medium new potatoes, sliced
1 medium red onion, sliced
1 bunch broccoli, stems and tops roughly chopped
3 carrots, thinly sliced
¼ teaspoon dried oregano (optional)
4 tablespoons water
1 pound kielbasa *or* other smoked sausage, sliced

1. In a large skillet fry bacon until crisp. Drain, reserving 1 tablespoon fat.

2. Add butter to bacon fat in skillet and cook vegetables and oregano, covered, over medium-high heat for 5 minutes, stirring occasionally.

3. Add water, sliced sausage, and bacon, and cook until vegetables are tender and sausage is heated through (10 minutes).

Spinach Salad with Lemon-Soy Dressing

1 bunch spinach, washed and stems removed
6 green onions, sliced (¼ cup)
½ cup sliced radishes
1 cup bean sprouts (optional)
1 can (8 oz) pineapple chunks, drained (retain 1 tablespoon juice for dressing)
Lemon-Soy Dressing (recipe follows)

1. Chop or tear spinach into bite-size pieces.

2. Arrange other vegetables and fruit in groups on top of spinach.

Lemon-Soy Dressing

¼ cup salad oil
2 tablespoons lemon juice
2 tablespoons soy sauce
1 tablespoon pineapple juice
Pinch garlic powder (optional)

Combine all ingredients thoroughly.

Dark Rye with Melted Cheese

4 to 8 slices dark rye bread
¼ pound Cheddar, mozzarella, Swiss, jack, *or* Teleme cheese, sliced

1. Toast bread until firm.

2. Top with cheese and broil until cheese melts. Halve diagonally before serving.

Note: Thin slices of tomato, onion, or avocado make an attractive topping.

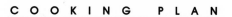

C O O K I N G   P L A N

1. Assemble all ingredients and cooking equipment.

2. Dice bacon and chop vegetables for one-pot dish.

3. Fry bacon. Cook vegetables.

4. Wash and chop spinach; chop other vegetables for salad and assemble.

5. Turn on broiler.

6. Add sausage and bacon to one-pot dish.

7. Toast bread; slice cheese; make salad dressing.

8. Top bread with cheese and broil.

To serve: Place salad and dressing on table. Slice bread and serve with one-pot dish.

35

Savory Sausage Cassoulet

Tomato-Cucumber-Cheese Salad

Garlic Bread

Beverage suggestion:
A dark or light beer

Savory Sausage Cassoulet

This is a quick, easy, and delicious version of the traditional cassoulet, a hearty French country favorite made by simmering dried small white beans and a variety of meats slowly for hours.

    1 tablespoon butter *or* salad oil
    1 pound Polish sausage, sliced
    ½ pound hot Italian sausage, sliced
    1 cup chopped red *or* yellow onion
    1 clove garlic, minced *or* pressed
    1 can (54 oz) pork and beans
    ¼ cup white wine
    ¼ teaspoon *each* black pepper and thyme
    2 pinches rosemary (ground between fingers)
    1 small bay leaf
      Green onion and diced pimiento, for garnish (optional)

1. Heat butter in a large skillet *or* heavy saucepan and sauté sausages. Remove from skillet and drain, reserving 1 table-spoon fat.

2. Add onion and garlic to skillet and sauté until soft. Add remaining ingredients, mix in sausage slices, and simmer 15 minutes.

3. Serve with Garlic Bread; garnish if desired.

Tomato-Cucumber-Cheese Salad

    2 fully ripe tomatoes, sliced
    1 medium red onion, thinly sliced
    1 cucumber, thinly sliced
    ½ pound feta cheese, crumbled
      Juice of 1 lemon
    2 to 3 tablespoons olive oil
      Salt and freshly ground black pepper

1. Top tomatoes with onion and cucumber slices.

2. Mix together cheese, lemon juice, and olive oil; season to taste.

3. Pour dressing over salad.

Simple French fare is highlighted by arrangement and garnish. Little touches, such as topping each of the individual casseroles with a slice of the garlic bread, are what turn everyday meals into something as special as this one.

Garlic Bread

    ½ loaf sweet *or* sourdough French bread
    ½ cup (1 cube) butter, softened
    2 to 3 cloves garlic, minced *or* pressed
    ¼ cup *each* minced fresh parsley and freshly grated Parmesan cheese

1. Preheat broiler.

2. Slice bread to desired thickness.

3. Mix together remaining ingredients and spread evenly over slices.

4. Broil slices on cookie sheet until golden and bubbly.

COOKING PLAN

1. Assemble all ingredients and cooking equipment.

2. Slice and chop all ingredients for cassoulet.

3. Sauté sausages.

4. Meanwhile, mince and grate ingredients for garlic bread spread and mix together.

5. Remove sausages; sauté onion and garlic.

6. Add remaining ingredients to cassoulet.

7. Prepare salad and dressing.

8. Turn on broiler.

9. Slice bread and spread with seasoned butter. Broil.

To serve: Place salad on table; serve cassoulet and bread.

Herbed Lamb Patties

Matchstick Potatoes

Carrots Purée

Sliced Beefsteak Tomatoes

Wine suggestion:
Merlot

Herbed Lamb Patties

- 1 tablespoon olive oil
- 1 bunch green onions, sliced
- 1½ to 2 pounds ground lamb
- ¼ teaspoon black pepper
- ½ teaspoon dried thyme *or* basil
- 1 tablespoon minced fresh *or* 1 teaspoon crushed dried rosemary
- 1 tablespoon minced parsley
- 2 teaspoons lemon juice
  Bottled mint sauce

1. Heat oil in a small skillet and sauté green onions.

2. In a bowl, thoroughly combine sautéed onion with remaining ingredients (except mint sauce).

3. Form lamb mixture into 4 patties and pan-fry or broil 5 minutes per side, or until done to taste.

4. Serve with mint sauce.

VARIATION

Nutted Lamb Patties with Bacon
Add ⅓ cup chopped nutmeats to ground lamb with onions and seasonings. Form into 4 patties. Broil first side 5 minutes. Turn patties and broil 3 minutes longer. Top *each* with a slice of Cheddar cheese and a slice of partially cooked bacon. Broil 2 to 3 minutes longer or until cheese is melted and bacon is crisp.

Matchstick Potatoes

- 3 large potatoes, scrubbed and sliced into matchstick-size pieces
  Water
  Vegetable oil, to a depth of ¼ inch in skillet

1. Bring enough water to boil in a saucepan to just cover potatoes and parboil potatoes 2 minutes. Drain thoroughly on paper towels.

1. Heat oil until hot but not smoking. (A piece of potato should rise immediately to the surface and bob about.) Add potatoes and fry until golden (4 to 5 minutes).

3. Drain on paper towels.

Delicately herbed lamb patties with the traditional mint sauce are a refreshing change from broiled ground beef. And for a variation on routine vegetables, try the Matchstick Potatoes and the Carrots Purée. Familiar foods served with flair!

Carrots Purée

- 1 pound small carrots, sliced thinly (3 cups)
- 2 tablespoons butter
- 2 tablespoons water
- 1 cup whipping cream
- 1 to 2 tablespoons dry sherry
- ¼ teaspoon *each* nutmeg and cinnamon

1. Melt butter in a large skillet; add carrots and water and steam, covered, until soft (5 to 8 minutes).

2. Combine carrots with remaining ingredients in blender and blend until smooth. Reheat if necessary.

Sliced Beefsteak Tomatoes

- 3 large beefsteak tomatoes
- ⅓ cup olive oil
- ¼ cup lemon juice
- 1 tablespoon *each* fresh *or* ½ teaspoon dried basil and rosemary

1. Slice tomatoes.

2. Whisk together remaining ingredients and pour over tomatoes. Let stand at room temperature until serving.

C O O K I N G   P L A N

1. Assemble all ingredients and cooking equipment.

2. Chop and measure ingredients for lamb patties. Sauté onion; form patties and set aside.

3. Slice potatoes and carrots.

4. Steam carrots and heat water for potatoes.

5. Slice tomatoes and top with dressing.

6. Parboil potatoes; drain.

7. Blend carrots and reheat.

8. Pan-fry or broil lamb patties.

9. Heat oil for potatoes. Just before turning patties, add test potato to oil.

10. Turn patties and fry potatoes.

To serve: Drain potatoes on paper towels. Top patties with mint sauce; serve with carrots and potatoes.

37

Curried Lamb and Vegetables

Bulgar Wheat

Endive-and-Mushroom Salad
with Sherried Mustard Dressing

Wine suggestion:
Gewürztraminer

Curried Lamb and Vegetables

- 1 tablespoon butter
- 1 to 3 teaspoons curry powder
- 1 teaspoon freshly grated or ¼ teaspoon ground ginger
- 2 to 3 cloves garlic, minced
- 1 medium red onion, chopped
- 1 pound ground lamb
- ½ pound (20 medium) mushrooms, sliced
  Half a green pepper, seeded and chopped
- 1 stalk celery, diced
- ½ cup grated carrot
  Lime wedges, for garnish

1. Melt butter over medium-high heat in a large, heavy skillet. Add curry powder, ginger, garlic, and onion, and sauté 30 seconds.

Accompany this spicy curry with colorful condiments: raisins, coconut, chutney, sliced almonds or chopped peanuts, chopped green onion, grated carrot, and plain yogurt.

2. Add lamb and brown lightly. Stir in vegetables and cook until tender (6 to 8 minutes). Garnish with lime wedges.

Bulgar Wheat

- 2 tablespoons oil
- 1 cup bulgar wheat
- 2 cups hot water or 1 cup each chicken broth and hot water
  Salt and freshly ground pepper to taste

1. Heat oil in a large skillet and sauté bulgar until golden.

2. Add hot liquid and salt and pepper and bring to a boil over high heat. Cover, reduce heat, and simmer until all liquid is absorbed (15 minutes).

Endive-and-Mushroom Salad with Sherried Mustard Dressing

- 12 medium or 8 large mushrooms, stems trimmed
- 2 heads endive or 1 head escarole, torn
- 2 green onions, chopped
- ½ cup plain yogurt
- 1½ teaspoons Dijon-style mustard
- 1 to 2 tablespoons sherry

1. Arrange mushrooms on endive.

2. Mix together onion, yogurt, mustard, and sherry. Spoon over salad.

C O O K I N G   P L A N

1. Assemble all ingredients and cooking equipment.

2. Sauté bulgar; add liquid and reduce heat.

3. Chop and measure ingredients for curried lamb.

4. Begin cooking curried lamb.

5. Prepare salad and dressing.

6. Assemble and chop desired condiments.

To serve: Place condiments and salad on table. Top bulgar with curried lamb.

Loin Lamb Chops with Juniper Sauce

Confetti Couscous

Brussels Sprouts

Wine suggestion:
French Côtes-du-Rhône or Beaujolais

Loin Lamb Chops with Juniper Sauce

The New Zealand lamb now available in many supermarkets makes this and other lamb dishes more affordable. Thinner chops, such as round-bone or shoulder, can also be prepared in this way. Simply reduce the broiling time to 4 or 5 minutes per side. Juniper berries are an intriguing alternative to the classic mint sauce.

    4 loin lamb chops (¾ to 1 in. thick)
    2 cloves garlic, minced
    1 tablespoon juniper berries, crushed
      Salt and freshly ground pepper to
      taste
      Juniper Sauce (recipe follows)

1. Rub chops with a paste of the garlic, juniper berries, and salt and pepper.

2. Broil chops 4 inches from heat source until done to taste (6 to 8 minutes per side for slightly pink, juicy meat). Line broiler with foil to collect drippings, which should be added to sauce.

3. While chops cook, prepare Juniper Sauce.

4. Spoon a little sauce over each chop; serve remainder separately.

Juniper Sauce

    ½ cup beef broth
    ⅔ cup dry red wine
    1 clove garlic, minced
    1 tablespoon juniper berries, crushed
    1 tablespoon red currant jelly
      Drippings from lamb chops
    1 tablespoon cornstarch
    2 tablespoons water
      Salt and freshly ground pepper
      to taste

1. In a small saucepan over medium-high heat, bring broth, wine, garlic, and berries to a boil. Reduce heat and simmer 6 minutes.

2. Stir in red currant jelly and drippings from chops.

3. Blend cornstarch and water in small bowl; stir into sauce.

4. Return sauce to a boil, and season.

Confetti Couscous

    3 cups chicken broth
    2 cups couscous
    3 green onions, thinly sliced
    3 to 4 tablespoons toasted pine nuts
      or sliced almonds
    ½ cup thinly sliced fresh mushrooms

1. Bring broth to a boil, add remaining ingredients, and stir.

2. Immediately remove from heat, cover, and let stand until liquid is absorbed (5 minutes).

Brussels Sprouts

      Water
    1 pound Brussels sprouts
    ¼ cup finely chopped red or green
      onion
    2 tablespoons butter
      Salt and freshly ground pepper

1. Bring to a boil enough water to just cover sprouts.

2. Trim off ends of sprouts and cut an X in the stem of each to speed cooking.

3. Add sprouts to boiling water, reduce heat, and simmer, uncovered, until tender (10 to 15 minutes). Drain and set aside.

4. In the same saucepan, cook onion in butter until soft (5 minutes). Cover pan to speed cooking.

5. Add sprouts, reheat, and season to taste.

C O O K I N G   P L A N

1. Assemble all ingredients and cooking equipment.

2. Heat broiler.

3. Wash and score sprouts; heat water. Mince garlic, crush berries, and measure other ingredients for chops and sauce.

4. Slice onions and mushrooms for couscous. Chop onions for sprouts.

5. Add sprouts to boiling water.

6. Season chops and broil. Prepare sauce.

7. Turn chops, adding drippings to sauce.

8. Heat broth for couscous and prepare dish.

9. Drain sprouts; sauté onion and return sprouts to pan.

To serve: Drizzle chops with a little sauce; offer remainder separately. Fluff couscous and serve sprouts.

For an elegant summer dinner, grill the chops on the barbeque rather than broiling them.

Lamb Chops Provencal

Creamed Chard

Glazed Parsnips

Baguette or French Rolls

Wine suggestion:
French Beaujolais

Lamb Chops Provencal

This French country sauce is also excellent with pork or chicken, or as a topping for pasta or omelets. If you have a few extra minutes, double the recipe and freeze half for future use.

4 loin, round-bone, *or* shoulder lamb chops, trimmed
Provencal Sauce (recipe follows)
Chopped ripe olives, for garnish (optional)

1. Broil chops 4 inches from heat source 4 to 8 minutes per side, depending on thickness.

2. Top with Provencal Sauce and garnish with olives if desired.

Provencal Sauce

1 tablespoon olive oil
1 medium onion, finely chopped
2 cloves garlic, minced *or* pressed
1 can (16 oz) whole tomatoes, drained
1 green pepper, seeded and sliced
½ cup dry red wine

1. Heat oil in a large frying pan and sauté onion and garlic briefly. Crush tomatoes and add to fryng pan; sauté briefly.

2. Add green pepper and wine and simmer 15 minutes.

3. Serve over broiled chops.

Creamed Chard

2 tablespoons butter
2 bunches chard (leaves only), washed and chopped
2 tablespoons water
1 package (3 oz) cream cheese, at room temperature
⅛ teaspoon nutmeg
Salt and pepper to taste

1. Melt butter in a large frying pan over medium-high heat. Add chard, water, and cream cheese, broken into chunks.

2. Cover and cook 4 minutes, or until chard is tender.

3. Add seasonings and mix well.

Chard and parsnips are delicious, low-cost vegetables. Try these tasty ways of preparing them and you'll want to add these little-used foods to your cooking repertoire. Like so many of the sauces in this book, this spicy Provençal can be used with other entrées.

Glazed Parsnips

1½ pounds (8 to 10) medium parsnips, trimmed and peeled
Boiling water
2 tablespoons *each* butter and brandy
1 tablespoon brown sugar *or* honey

1. Cook parsnips in a large skillet in enough boiling water to cover until just tender (10 to 15 minutes).

2. Drain and add remaining ingredients.

3. Sauté over medium-high heat 5 minutes, shaking pan occasionally to glaze parsnips on all sides.

COOKING PLAN

1. Assemble all ingredients and cooking equipment.

2. Chop ingredients for Provençal Sauce, and olives for garnish. Wash and chop chard. Clean parsnips.

3. Heat broiler, and water for parsnips.

4. Sauté vegetables for sauce. Add remaining ingredients and simmer.

5. Cook parsnips. Place chops in broiler.

6. Check chops and turn when ready.

7. Cook chard.

8. Drain parsnips and glaze. Season chard.

To serve: Spoon sauce over chops; garnish. Serve vegetables.

Casserole of Noodles Italian-Style

Fruited Romaine Salad

Round Loaf or Bread Sticks

Wine suggestion:
Italian Barolo

With the proper staging, a "noodle casserole" can be elevated to elegance—serve it on a platter against a background of candles and flowers. The salad features oranges and kiwi with crisp greens, and the crusty round Italian loaf tops off yet another great meal.

Casserole of Noodles Italian-Style

This basic pasta casserole can be varied by adding diced leftover beef or chicken, baby shrimp, or cooked vegetables such as broccoli, peas, or carrots.

    1 pound medium noodles
    4 quarts boiling water
    3 eggs, well beaten
    ¼ cup whipping cream
    ¼ cup chopped fresh parsley
    ¼ cup minced onion
    1 cup freshly grated Parmesan cheese
    ½ pound (20 medium) mushrooms, sliced
    1 tablespoon *Fines Herbes*
      Parsley sprigs, for garnish

1. Preheat oven to 375°F.

2. Cook noodles in boiling water until just tender (5 to 7 minutes); drain.

3. Meanwhile, combine all other ingredients.

4. Place noodles in greased casserole dish; pour sauce over noodles and stir to mix.

5. Bake 20 minutes; garnish with parsley.

Fruited Romaine Salad

    1 bunch romaine
    2 large carrots
    2 oranges
    2 or 3 kiwi fruit
      Cruets of oil and vinegar

1. Wash and chop romaine.

2. Scrub carrots and slice into long, thin strips using a vegetable peeler.

3. Peel and slice oranges and kiwi fruit.

4. Arrange vegetable and fruits on lettuce.

Round Loaf or Bread Sticks

Warm a round Italian or French loaf in 350°F oven for 10 minutes, or serve crunchy bread sticks with the casserole.

C O O K I N G P L A N

1. Assemble all ingredients and cooking equipment.

2. Heat water for pasta.

3. Preheat oven to 375°F.

4. Chop parsley, onions, and mushrooms and grate cheese for casserole. Combine with other ingredients.

5. As soon as water boils, add pasta.

6. Drain pasta and assemble casserole. Place in oven.

7. Make salad and wash parsley for casserole garnish.

8. Warm bread.

To serve: Place bread or bread sticks, salad, cruets, and casserole on table.

Pasta with Choice of Sauce

Garden Patch Green Salad

Rosemary Loaf

Wine suggestion:
Italian red or white wine

Pasta with Choice of Sauce

Pasta is tastiest made from scratch using freshly milled flour, but this is not an option for the cook who only has 30 minutes. However, fresh pasta can be purchased in Italian delis and gourmet food stores. When cooking fresh pasta, reduce the cooking time by up to half.

This recipe calls for dry pasta. Experiment with the new shapes, colors, and flavors now available at your grocery.

- 4 quarts water
- 1 tablespoon salt
- 2 tablespoons olive oil
- 1 pound spaghetti, noodles, *or* macaroni
  Pasta sauce (recipes follow)

1. In a large kettle, bring salted water to a rapid boil. Add oil and then pasta. Return to boil.

2. Cook, uncovered, until just tender (7 to 10 minutes, depending on size and shape of pasta). Stir occasionally with a long-handled fork to prevent sticking.

3. Drain in colander. Do not rinse.

4. Top with your choice of sauce.

PASTA SAUCES

Parmesan Noodles

Melt ¼ cup butter in a medium saucepan. Add 1 cup freshly grated Parmesan cheese, ½ cup half-and-half *or* evaporated skim milk, and salt and pepper to taste. Pour over cooked pasta, toss, and garnish with minced fresh parsley.

Mushroom Sauce

In 2 tablespoons butter *or* olive oil, sauté 1 pound roughly chopped mushrooms, ⅓ cup chopped green onion, and 1 to 2 minced cloves garlic. Stir in ½ cup white wine *or* chicken broth, 1 bay leaf, and ½ teaspoon *each* basil, oregano, salt, and Worcestershire sauce. Simmer 10 to 15 minutes. Pour over cooked pasta, toss, and top with grated Parmesan cheese.

David's Curried Cream Sauce

Melt 2 tablespoons butter in a medium saucepan; add 2 tablespoons flour and cook, stirring, until bubbly. Blend in 2 cups half-and-half *or* evaporated skim milk and ½ to 1 teaspoon curry powder. Bring to a boil and cook until slightly thickened. Fold in ½ to 1 pound thawed tiny shrimp and ½ to ¾ cup freshly grated Romano *or* Parmesan cheese. Pour over cooked pasta, toss, and garnish with additional grated Romano and lemon wedges. Clams, scallops, *or* crab may be substituted for the shrimp.

J.C.'s Four-Cheese Favorite

Toss ¼ pound *each* finely cubed Gruyère and Fontina cheese and 1 cup *each* freshly grated Parmesan and Romano cheese with 2 tablespoons flour. Heat ¼ cup butter and 1 cup half-and-half *or* evaporated skim milk in a heavy-bottomed saucepan until butter melts. Gradually stir in cheeses and cook over medium heat until sauce is smooth. Add 1 tablespoon chopped fresh basil, rosemary, or thyme *or* 1 teaspoon any dried herb. Pour sauce over cooked pasta and toss quickly with two spoons. Just before serving, add an additional ½ to ¾ cup coarsely grated Parmesan cheese, and toss to mix.

Fettuccini Amandine

Mix together ⅔ cup coarsely ground dry-roasted almonds, 6 to 8 ounces diced prosciutto (optional), ¼ cup *each* shredded provolone and Monterey jack cheese, 2 to 3 tablespoons half-and-half beaten with 1 egg, 1 minced clove garlic, and ½ teaspoon Italian herb seasoning. Return drained pasta to kettle, add sauce ingredients, and toss lightly over medium heat until cheese melts. Garnish with freshly ground black pepper, minced fresh parsley, and chopped almonds.

Italian Sausage and Pepper Sauce

Sauté ½ pound *each* hot and sweet Italian pork sausages, casings removed, *or* 1 pound bulk sausage until brown. Drain all but 1 tablespoon fat. Add 1 green pepper, seeded and cut in strips; ¼ cup sliced red onion; 1 minced clove garlic; 1 teaspoon oregano leaves; ½ teaspoon *each* basil and thyme; ½ teaspoon salt; and ¼ teaspoon freshly ground pepper. Sauté until pepper and onion are tender (10 minutes), stirring frequently. Stir in 1 can (28 oz) plum tomatoes (and liquid), breaking up with a fork. Simmer 5 minutes. Pour over drained pasta, toss, and top with grated Parmesan cheese.

Garden Patch Green Salad

- 2 heads butter or red lettuce; escarole; or spinach *or* a combination of any of these
- 3 ripe tomatoes, sliced
- 1 cucumber, sliced
- 1 zucchini, thinly sliced
- 2 carrots, grated or cut in sticks
- 1½ cups sliced fresh mushrooms
  One of these fruits:
- ½ cup seedless grapes
- 1 can (11½ oz) unsweetened mandarin orange segments
- 1 or 2 kiwi fruit, peeled and sliced
- 1 red *or* yellow apple, cored and thinly sliced
  Your favorite dressing

Gently toss ingredients in a bowl. Dress immediately before serving.

Rosemary Loaf

- 1 round (1 lb) French or Italian loaf
- ½ cup (1 cube) softened butter
- 1 tablespoon chopped fresh *or* 1 teaspoon dried rosemary, crumbled
- 2 to 3 tablespoons minced fresh parsley
- ¼ cup grated Romano *or* Parmesan cheese

1. Preheat broiler.

2. Slice bread.

3. Combine remaining ingredients thoroughly. Spread evenly among slices.

4. Broil until cheese is bubbly and golden brown.

C O O K I N G   P L A N

1. Assemble all ingredients and cooking equipment.

2. Chop, mince, or grate ingredients for sauce of your choice. If sauce must simmer, prepare now.

3. Wash and slice salad ingredients and assemble salad.

4. Heat water for pasta. Preheat broiler.

5. Prepare rosemary loaf but do not broil.

6. Cook pasta. If sauce does not require simmering, prepare now.

7. Place bread in broiler.

8. Drain pasta and, depending on choice of sauce, combine or top with sauce.

To serve: Dress salad, remove bread from broiler, and garnish pasta.

Oh, the infinite shapes and tastes of pastas and sauces! Beginning with the ideas in this menu, experiment and enjoy to your heart's content. One taste of David's Curried Cream Sauce and it will be love at first bite. Ease and economy further the appeal of pasta dinners.

An economical vegetarian choice that's often served in Italian trattorias. A light touch with the sauce keeps the eggplant from being overwhelmed. Baked in foil, flavored with sherry, and topped with sour cream, the mushrooms are a mouth-watering addition to this meal.

Vermicelli

- 2 quarts water
- 1 teaspoon salt
- 8 ounces Italian vermicelli
- 1 tablespoon olive oil

1. Bring salted water to a boil.

2. Add vermicelli and oil and cook, uncovered, until tender but firm (3 to 5 minutes).

3. Drain and serve topped with Parmigiana Sauce.

Baked Mushrooms

- ¾ pound (30 medium) mushrooms
- ¼ cup minced fresh parsley
- 2 to 3 tablespoons dry sherry
  Salt and freshly ground pepper to taste
  Sour cream

1. Rinse mushrooms and trim stem ends. Place on piece of foil large enough to enclose them completely.

2. Top with remaining ingredients (except sour cream) and seal package tightly so that juices won't leak.

3. Bake in 450°F oven for 20 minutes.

4. Top each serving with a dollop of sour cream, or place mushrooms in serving dish and fold in sour cream.

C O O K I N G P L A N

1. Assemble all ingredients and cooking equipment.

2. Preheat oven to 450°F. Heat water in steamer.

3. Chop vegetables for sauce and sauté.

4. Prepare mushrooms; place in oven.

5. Slice eggplant and place in steamer.

6. Add remaining ingredients to sauce. Heat water for vermicelli.

7. Blot eggplant; coat and sauté.

8. Slice cheese; assemble eggplant dish.

9. Add vermicelli to boiling water.

To serve: Drain vermicelli and top with sauce, garnish mushrooms with sour cream, and serve eggplant.

42

Eggplant Parmigiana

Vermicelli

Baked Mushrooms

Wine suggestion:
Trebbiano (white) or Valpolicella (red)

Eggplant Parmigiana

This hearty dish is a vegetarian classic. The sauce goes well with many pasta, egg, and meat dishes.

- 1 large eggplant, unpeeled
  Boiling water, for steaming
- ½ cup flour
- 1 egg, beaten with ¼ cup milk
- ½ cup dried bread crumbs, wheat germ, *or* cracker meal
- ½ cup olive oil
  Parmigiana Sauce (recipe follows)
- ½ pound mozzarella *or* Swiss cheese, sliced

1. Wash eggplant and cut into ½-inch-thick slices.

2. Steam over boiling water for 5 minutes. Press each slice firmly between paper towels to remove moisture.

3. Coat each slice well, first with flour, then with egg-milk mixture, and finally with bread crumbs.

4. Divide oil between 2 large skillets and sauté eggplant over medium-high heat until golden brown on both sides. Drain slices on paper towels if desired. Discard oil.

5. Return eggplant to skillet, cover with Parmigiana Sauce, and top with cheese. Cover skillet and cook until cheese melts (5 minutes).

Parmigiana Sauce

- 1 small red onion, chopped
- 1 large clove garlic, minced
- ¼ cup diced green pepper (optional)
- 1 tablespoon olive oil
- 1 can (28 oz) Italian plum tomatoes
- 1 tablespoon minced fresh parsley (optional)
- ½ teaspoon *each* dried basil, thyme, and oregano

1. Sauté onion, garlic, and green pepper in oil until softened.

2. Add tomatoes, squeezing between fingers to break up (or chop in can using 2 knives), their liquid, and herbs. Simmer, covered, 10 to 15 minutes.

3. Use half the sauce for eggplant; serve the remainder over the vermicelli.

Skillet Vegetarian Delight

Herbed Brown Rice

Fruit and Cheese Board

Wine suggestion:
Chablis or Vin Rosé

Stir-frying is a natural for the 30-minute cook. Chopping commands most of the time — and then it all comes together quickly in a one-pot meal. Get everyone into the act and you'll have a colorful, tasty meal on the table in no time, as well as a party atmosphere!

Skillet Vegetarian Delight

The secret to this stir-fried dish is not to overcook it. The colorful ingredients make a quick and economical meal.

3	tablespoons olive oil
1	to 3 cloves garlic, minced *or* pressed
2	teaspoons grated fresh ginger root
1	small red onion, sliced
2	green *or* red peppers, seeded and diced (or 1 of each)
¼	pound green beans, sliced diagonally in 1-inch lengths
1	carrot, coarsely grated
¾	pound (30 medium) mushrooms, sliced
1	small bunch Chinese bok choy *or* chard
1	zucchini, sliced
¼	pound tofu (soybean curd), cubed
1½	teaspoons dried basil
½	teaspoon dried thyme
2	tablespoons minced fresh parsley
1	teaspoon lemon juice
2	to 3 tablespoons soy sauce, or to taste

1. Heat oil, garlic, and ginger in a large skillet or wok.

2. Add onion, peppers, beans, and carrot and stir-fry over high heat 4 minutes.

3. Add mushrooms, bok choy, zucchini, tofu, and herbs. Pour lemon juice and soy sauce over vegetables and stir-fry until tender (4 to 5 minutes).

4. Serve over rice.

Herbed Brown Rice

2	cups water
1	tablespoon butter
1	cup short-grain brown rice
1½	teaspoons dried basil
¼	teaspoon dried thyme
1	teaspoon minced fresh parsley

1. Bring water, butter, and rice to a boil. Add remaining ingredients and stir *once*.

2. Reduce heat, cover, and simmer until all water is absorbed (20 to 25 minutes).

Fruit and Cheese Board

Serve this with the entrée or as an appetizing first course.

2	red *or* yellow Delicious apples, cored and cut in wedges
1	bunch red *or* white grapes
1	orange, cut in wedges
½	pound Cheddar *or* Monterey jack cheese
1	dozen whole-grain crackers

Arrange fruit, cheese, and crackers on a cutting board.

C O O K I N G   P L A N

1. Assemble all ingredients and cooking equipment.

2. Start rice.

3. Slice, chop, and mince all vegetables.

4. Prepare fruit and cheese board.

5. Stir-fry vegetables.

To serve: Place fruit and cheese board on table. Spoon vegetables over rice.

44

Jambalaya One-Pot Meal

Citrus Salad with Yogurt Dressing

Wine suggestion:
Rosé or Pinot Noir Blanc

Jambalaya One-Pot Meal

Although there are a number of ingredients to chop, this New Orleans-style dish needs no attention while it cooks. Once the jambalaya is assembled, you can prepare the salad at a leisurely pace.

The two variations show how versatile rice is as the basis for a one-pot meal. Develop some variations of your own that incorporate your family's favorites. Try a vegetarian version, create a new entrée from turkey breast strips and nuts, or concoct a fish and fruit dish.

```
2   tablespoons olive oil
2   cloves garlic, minced or pressed
½   cup chopped onion
1   stalk celery, sliced
1   medium green pepper, seeded
    and cut in strips
1   cup long-grain white rice
1   can (16 oz) stewed tomatoes
1   cup water
⅛   teaspoon tabasco sauce (optional)
½   cup chopped cooked ham
    (optional)
8   thin slices chorizo or other spicy hard
    sausage
1   teaspoon dried thyme or oregano
1   teaspoon salt
    Freshly ground black pepper
1   pound medium-size raw (in shells) or
    frozen shrimp
```

1. In a large skillet or paella pan, heat oil and sauté garlic, onion, celery, and green pepper just until softened (about 3 minutes).

2. Add remaining ingredients (except shrimp). Bring to a boil, reduce heat, cover, and simmer 15 minutes.

3. Quickly add shrimp, cover, and cook 5 minutes longer, or until rice is tender and shrimp have turned pink.

4. Toss with a fork to fluff rice and to distribute shrimp.

VARIATIONS

Paella One-Pot Meal

In 2 tablespoons olive oil, sauté 2 minced cloves garlic, ½ cup chopped onion, and 2 hot or mild chorizos (casings removed and broken into pieces) for 3 to 5 minutes. Add 1 cup long-grain white rice, 2 cups chicken broth, 1 whole boned chicken breast (cut in strips or bite-size pieces), ⅛ teaspoon saffron or ¼ teaspoon turmeric, 1 teaspoon salt, and freshly ground pepper to taste. Bring to a boil, reduce heat, cover, and simmer 15 minutes. Then add half a 20-ounce bag frozen petite peas or 1 can (16 oz) drained artichoke hearts and 1 pound medium-size raw (deveined) or frozen shrimp. Cover and cook 5 minutes longer. You can also add 8 fresh clams or mussels with the shrimp (reduce shrimp to ½ pound). Cook shellfish until shells open.

Gingered Chicken-Rice One-Pot Meal

In 2 tablespoons oil, sauté 1 minced clove garlic, ½ cup chopped onion, 1 cup sliced fresh mushrooms, and 1 tablespoon grated fresh ginger just until softened (3 minutes). Add 1 cup long-grain white rice; 2 cups chicken broth (or 1¾ cups broth and ¼ cup mandarin juice if you will add oranges), 2 whole boned chicken breasts (cut in strips or bite-size pieces), ½ cup toasted slivered almonds or chopped walnuts, ½ cup raisins, 1 teaspoon salt, and freshly ground pepper to taste. Bring to a boil, reduce heat, cover, and simmer 20 minutes. If you wish, add 1 can (11½ oz) drained mandarin orange segments after 15 minutes.

Citrus Salad with Yogurt Dressing

Slices of papaya, nectarine, mango, or other fresh fruits can be substituted for the oranges.

```
2   small heads butter or Bibb lettuce
1   avocado, sliced
1   orange, peeled, seeded, and sliced
    or 1 can (11½ oz) mandarin orange
    segments, drained
    Yogurt Dressing (recipe follows)
```

1. Wash and dry lettuce and separate into leaves.

2. Top with avocado and orange slices and a dollop of dressing.

Yogurt Dressing

```
1   cup plain yogurt
¼   cup orange juice
2   teaspoons grated orange peel
    Powdered sugar to taste
    Dash ground cloves
```

Mix all ingredients and let dressing stand to blend flavors.

COOKING PLAN

1. Assemble all ingredients and cooking equipment.

2. Chop vegetables for jambalaya and sauté, adding to pan as they are chopped.

3. Slice meats and clean shrimp.

4. Add remaining ingredients to jambalaya and cover.

5. Prepare salad and dressing.

6. Add shrimp to jambalaya.

To serve: Dress salad. Gently toss jambalaya.

A seafood lover's delight, this light meal is much less expensive than eating out. A paella pan enhances the display, but is not essential. And, like most one-pot meals, the variations and modifications are almost limitless. Be sure to try the orange-flavored yogurt dressing on the citrus salad, to complete this colorful meal filled with texture and taste surprises.

A hearty supper soup such as this one is great for a cold and hungry crowd, whether they've been skiing, tramping in the woods, or fighting their way through the cold urban jungle. Economy and ease characterize this last of fifty 30-minute meals.

50

Mexican Bean Soup

Fruited Green Salad
with Mexican Dressing

Herb Bread

Beverage suggestion:
Mexican beer

Mexican Bean Soup

Toppings such as sour cream or plain yogurt, chopped cilantro or green onion, diced avocado, grated cheese, and salsa add an authentic finishing touch to this hearty, low-cost soup.

  2 tablespoons butter
¼ cup chopped red or yellow onion
  2 carrots, diced
  2 medium zucchini, cubed
  1 can (17 oz) spicy pinto or refried beans
  1 can (14½ oz) chicken broth
  1 whole cooked chicken breast, diced

1. Melt butter in soup pot and sauté onion, carrots, and zucchini until tender (6 to 8 minutes).

2. Add remaining ingredients and simmer 10 minutes.

3. Serve with choice of toppings.

Fruited Green Salad with Mexican Dressing

¼ head *each* iceberg and romaine lettuce
  1 head butter lettuce
  6 large radishes, sliced
  1 large tomato, cut in wedges
  4 to 6 large mushrooms, sliced
  1 avocado, sliced
  3 fresh peaches, sliced *or* 1 can (16 oz) sliced Cling peaches, drained
    Mexican Dressing (recipe follows)
    Shredded sharp Cheddar cheese, for garnish

1. Wash lettuce and cut in bite-size pieces. Place in large salad bowl.

2. Arrange fruits and vegetables over lettuce.

3. When ready to serve, add dressing, toss, and garnish with cheese.

Mexican Dressing

½ cup mild *or* hot taco sauce
¼ cup *each* red wine vinegar and salad oil
  1 tablespoon *each* minced parsley and diced green chiles (optional)
  1 teaspoon minced cilantro
  1 teaspoon minced fresh *or* ¼ teaspoon dried oregano

Combine all ingredients thoroughly.

Herb Bread

  1 loaf French bread
½ cup (1 cube) butter, softened
⅛ teaspoon cumin
  1 tablespoon minced fresh *or* ½ teaspoon dried oregano
  2 tablespoons salsa

1. Halve bread lengthwise (parallel to crusts).

2. Mix butter and other ingredients and spread on cut sides of bread. Slice halves crosswise — to but not through crust — for single, pull-apart servings.

3. Broil until golden (2 to 3 minutes).

C O O K I N G   P L A N

1. Assemble all ingredients and cooking equipment.

2. Dice vegetables for soup and sauté.

3. Prepare salad and dressing.

4. Add remaining ingredients to soup.

5. Preheat broiler and prepare herb bread.

6. Chop toppings for soup and place in small bowls.

7. Put bread in broiler.

To serve: Place toppings for soup on table. Dress salad. Remove bread from broiler, and ladle soup into bowls.

Mai
with
a sw
is a
reci
in th
time

Add
bini
crea
adul
mak
thes
froz

Prep

The
Over
them
grand
or fre
equiv

Mak
Spool
(molc
cooki
For
olate

The Big (

No-Bake Cookies

Both of these cookies are simple to make, can be kept in the refrigerator for up to a week, or can be frozen for longer storage. Add them to the lunch box frozen and they will have thawed by lunch time. They're also great energizers for hiking or skiing.

Preparation time: 10 minutes

Jewel Drops

1 cup *each* dried dates, apricots, prunes, and raisins
½ cup (4 oz package) chopped nuts
1 teaspoon pumpkin pie spice
½ cup any instant hot cereal

1. In a food processor, combine all ingredients, except cereal and process until blended (2 to 3 minutes).

2. Shape into walnut-size balls and roll in cereal. (Grease your hands with a little butter or salad oil to make this easier.) Refrigerate or freeze.

Yield: 3 dozen

Healthy Chews

½ cup butter
1 cup honey
¼ cup carob powder
1 cup grated apple
¼ teaspoon salt
2 tablespoons wheat germ
½ teaspoon pumpkin pie spice *or* cinnamon
3 cups quick cooking oatmeal
½ cup *each* chopped dried dates and apricots
½ cup *each* chopped walnuts and flaked coconut
1 teaspoon vanilla

1. Melt butter in a large saucepan, add next 7 ingredients, stir, and heat through.

2. Add fruits, nuts, coconut, and vanilla and mix well.

3. Drop by heaping teaspoonfuls onto a buttered baking sheet or waxed paper. Refrigerate or freeze.

Yield: 5 dozen

Frozen Desserts

All of these desserts are light, refreshing, and appealing to the eye. Although they must be chilled before serving, they are quick and easy to prepare. Put them in the freezer before sitting down to the meal and most will be ready when you are. Or, chill overnight and enjoy them the next day.

In the recipes that call for them, you can choose between fresh or frozen berries. Although fresh are tastiest for eating whole, their availability is limited and they can be costly. Unless you have a source of inexpensive fresh berries, don't hesitate to use the frozen ones. They produce excellent results in these desserts. When blended, their texture is often thicker than the fresh — and the flavor may be more intense. And, frozen berries let you make these desserts all year long.

Papaya Ice

This sunny dessert is light and different. You can also serve it with a wedge of melon for breakfast on a hot summer morning. Fresh pineapple, mango, or peaches may be substituted for the papaya. And, experiment with frozen fruits or combinations of fruits for variety.

1 cup sugar
1 cup water
Juice of one lime *or* lemon
4 papayas, peeled, seeded, and roughly chopped

1. In a saucepan, bring sugar and water to a boil. Place in freezer to chill (5 minutes).

2. In a blender or food processor, purée syrup, lime juice, and papaya. Pour into a shallow metal pan (for fast freezing). Freeze at least 20 minutes.

3. Serve in dessert dishes, or for a festive touch, in hollowed-out lemon or lime shells.

Note: Ice may be thawed slightly before serving and beaten with an electric mixer to a creamy slush.

Preparation time: 15 minutes
Freezing time: 20 minutes

Chocolate Mousse

You can make this mouth-watering mousse ahead and refrigerate it for up to 3 days.

8 ounces semisweet chocolate (preferably French Lanvin or Ghirardelli), broken into pieces
1 cup (2 cubes) sweet butter
¼ to ½ cup sugar (to taste)
6 eggs
2 to 3 tablespoons Cognac, Amaretto, *or* concentrated coffee
Whipping cream and crushed macaroons *or* almonds, for garnish (optional)

1. Melt chocolate in top of double boiler or in microwave oven.

2. With electric mixer, beat butter and sugar at high speed until light and fluffy.

3. Add chocolate and eggs, one at a time, beating until thoroughly blended. Stir in Cognac.

4. Spoon into soufflé dish or individual serving dishes and freeze 10 minutes. Cover and refrigerate until serving.

5. Garnish with whipped cream and macaroons if desired.

Preparation time: 10 minutes
Freezing time: 10 to 15 minutes

These frozen desserts range from light and refreshing to decadently rich. Pictured from left to right are the chocolate mousse and the strawberry, raspberry, and blueberry fruit mousses, with the golden papaya ice featured in back.

Fruit Mousse

  3 egg whites
  ¼ cup sugar
  2 pints fresh *or* 1 package (20 oz) frozen strawberries, raspberries, or blueberries, thawed and drained
  1 cup plain yogurt
  1 teaspoon vanilla *or* almond extract
    Kiwi fruit *or* ground almond macaroons, for garnish

1. With an electric mixer, beat whites at high speed until they form soft peaks. Gradually beat in sugar.

2. In a blender or food processor, purée fruit with yogurt and vanilla.

3. Fold fruit mixture into egg whites.

4. Divide mixture among 4 parfait glasses and freeze.

5. Garnish with slices of kiwi or sprinkle with ground macaroons before serving.

Preparation time: 15 minutes
Freezing time: 15 minutes

Variation: Purée fruit and vanilla, omitting yogurt. Whip 1 cup heavy cream; fold into fruit. Layer mousse with crushed cookies if desired, and garnish with fresh berries. (See raspberry mousse in the photograph above.)

Fruit-Cream Parfait

  8 ounces cream cheese, softened
  1 cup whipping cream
  ¼ cup powdered sugar
  1 to 2 teaspoons lemon juice
    Grated peel of 1 *each* orange and lemon
  2½ cups sliced fresh *or* frozen fruit
    Whipped cream *or* chopped nuts, for garnish

1. In an electric mixer, beat cream cheese and whipping cream on high speed until light and fluffy.

2. Reduce speed to low and add sugar, lemon juice, and citrus peel.

3. Layer ⅛ of the cream cheese mixture in each of 4 wine glasses. Top with ½ cup of fruit and ¼ of the remaining cream cheese. Chill in freezer 10 to 15 minutes.

4. Divide remaining ½ cup fruit among the 4 wine glasses and garnish as desired.

Preparation time: 10 minutes
Freezing time: 10 to 15 minutes

Desserts for Special Occasions

Here are some truly grand finales for a special meal, for entertaining, or for when you simply want something out of the ordinary. Most take only 10 to 15 minutes to prepare—and all are well worth the time.

Flaming Bananas Foster

You can substitute 4 large fresh peaches or pears or 2 papayas in this Caribbean dessert. If you substitute canned fruits, use some of their syrup to extend the sauce.

⅓ cup butter
⅓ cup firmly packed brown sugar or ¼ cup honey
4 bananas
3 tablespoons *each* rum and banana liqueur
2 cups praline *or* coffee ice cream

1. In a chafing dish or in a skillet on the stove, melt butter and sugar.

2. Quarter bananas lengthwise and crosswise. Toss gently in sauce to warm.

3. Divide ice cream among 4 parfait or wine glasses.

4. Add rum and liqueur to bananas; heat on high for 1 minute and ignite. Spoon sauce over ice cream.

Preparation time: 10 minutes

Figs with Flavored Ricotta

12 medium-size ripe fresh figs
1 cup ricotta cheese
1 teaspoon *each* grated lemon and orange peel
¾ teaspoon vanilla
¼ cup honey
Chopped pistachios, hazelnuts, *or* almonds, for garnish (optional)

1. Remove stem ends from figs. Cut each into a tulip shape by slicing into quarters from stem *almost* to blossom end. Press on stem end to open petals.

2. Whirl remaining ingredients in blender or food processor.

3. Stuff each fig with 2 tablespoons flavored ricotta.

4. Garnish with chopped nuts if desired.

Preparation time: 10 minutes

Pears with Melba Sauce

For a more substantial dessert, serve these colorful pears over ice cream or slices of purchased angel food cake.

½ cup water
¼ cup sugar
4 fresh pears, quartered and cored
1 pint fresh *or* 1 package (10 oz) frozen raspberries, thawed
2 teaspoons lemon juice
3 tablespoons powdered sugar (or to taste)
1 tablespoon kirsch (optional)
2 kiwi fruit, sliced (optional)

1. Mix water and sugar in saucepan. Bring to a boil, add pears, reduce heat, and simmer until fork-tender (10 minutes). Discard poaching liquid or save for poaching other fruit.

2. Meanwhile, purée raspberries in blender or processor and strain if desired. Stir in lemon juice, powdered sugar, and kirsch.

3. Remove pears to serving dish. Pour sauce over and garnish with kiwi slices if desired.

Preparation time: 15 minutes

Brandied Fruit Flambé

Make this elegant topping for ice cream or cheesecake with any fresh fruit. It can also be served on a bed of crushed macaroons. If you don't have a chafing dish, prepare the flambé in a saucepan or skillet.

½ cup *each* sugar and water
3 whole cloves
1 stick cinnamon, broken into pieces
2 cups fresh fruit, cut in bite-size pieces
2 cups ice cream
¼ cup Cognac

1. In chafing dish, bring sugar, water, cloves, and cinnamon to a boil; boil 5 minutes. Discard spices.

2. Add fruit and simmer until warmed through.

3. Divide ice cream among 4 parfait glasses.

4. Add Cognac to fruit, heat thoroughly and ignite, and spoon sauce over ice cream.

Preparation time: 15 minutes

For a showy finish to your 30-minute meal, try Flaming Bananas Foster. Any fruit can be substituted for the bananas, and you can pour this delicious sauce over ice cream or angel food cake.

Rosé Pears is an elegant yet easy dessert — poach fresh or canned pears, stuff with dried fruits and nuts or chocolate, and then float in a flavored chocolate bath or on a sea of vanilla cream.

Sweet Souffléed Omelet

¼ cup milk
4 egg yolks
1 tablespoon *each* Cognac *or* Grand Marnier and sugar
4 egg whites
1 tablespoon butter

Topping:
Powdered sugar
2 tablespoons orange juice
2 to 3 tablespoons Grand Marnier, warmed

1. Combine milk, yolks, Cognac, and sugar thoroughly with a fork.

2. Beat egg whites until stiff but not dry.

3. Stir ⅓ of the whites into yolk mixture. Fold in remainder of whites.

4. Melt butter in an ovenproof skillet over medium-high heat. Add batter and cover skillet.

5. As omelet cooks, slash with a knife to bottom crust to permit heat to penetrate.

6. After 5 minutes, remove lid and transfer omelet to 350°F oven until top is set (2 minutes).

7. Remove omelet from skillet and sprinkle with sugar and orange juice. Pour warm liqueur over or around it and ignite.

Preparation time: 15 minutes

TOPPING VARIATIONS

- Apricot-pineapple preserves.
- Sliced fresh fruit topped with powdered sugar or honey.
- Whole berries and sour or whipped cream mixed with a little grated lemon peel and juice.
- Amaretto, sliced almonds, and sweetened sour or whipped cream *or* ricotta cheese.
- Grand Marnier and orange slices.

Rosé Pears in Chocolate Bath

Poach the pears and mix the sauce ahead of time. Then, this elegant dessert can be quickly assembled just before serving.

2½ cups burgundy wine
⅓ cup sugar
½ stick cinnamon, broken
⅛ teaspoon coriander seed *or* 1/16 teaspoon ground coriander
3 whole cloves
Grated peel of half an orange
Grated peel of 1 lemon
4 Bartlett pears, peeled
1 can (5 oz) chocolate sauce
2 to 3 tablespoons Cognac, Grand Marnier, *or* almond liqueur
Mint sprigs, kiwi slices, *or* candied violet leaves, for garnish

1. Combine first 7 ingredients in saucepan. Bring to a boil and reduce heat.

2. Add pears and simmer until just tender (8 to 10 minutes).

3. With a slotted spoon, remove pears. (Halve and core if desired.) Place whole or halved pear upright in each of 4 champagne or sherbet glasses.

4. Mix chocolate sauce and Cognac. Pour around pears and garnish as desired.

Preparation time: 15 to 20 minutes

VARIATIONS

Nut-Filled Pears in Chocolate

Poach pears as directed. Halve pears horizontally, cutting in a sawtooth pattern to flute. Core, and stuff each half with a mixture of chopped nuts, raisins, dried dates, and dried apricots. Reassemble pears and surround each with chocolate sauce.

Rosé Pears with Vanilla Cream

Poach the pears as directed, but serve them on a "sea" of vanilla cream. Whip 1 carton (8 oz) heavy cream. Fold cream into 1 cup vanilla pudding flavored with 1 to 2 tablespoons Cognac. Place cream in bottom of serving glasses. (Wine glasses look elegant.) Top with pears and garnish with mint.

Rosé Pears and Ice Cream

Poach pears as directed, halve vertically, and core. Place a scoop of your favorite ice cream, sherbet, *or* frozen yogurt in each of 4 champagne or sherbet glasses. Lean 2 pear halves against each scoop.

Fruited Melon Meringue

4 egg whites
1 tablespoon sugar
2 small honeydew melons *or* cantaloupes, halved and seeded
2 cups ice cream *or* frozen yogurt
2 peaches *or* pears, sliced

1. Preheat oven to 450°F.

2. With an electric mixer, whip whites and sugar until stiff. Pipe or spoon in 4 mounds onto baking sheet lined with cooking parchment. Bake until lightly browned (2 to 3 minutes). Cool.

3. Place melon halves in serving bowls. Fill with ice cream; place fruit slices on top.

4. Top each melon half with a meringue.

Preparation time: 15 minutes

Quick Breakfasts & Lunches

Even if you eat breakfast on the run or pack lunch in a bag, these meals can be tasty and appealing. Try the fruit shakes and soups; breakfast sandwiches; omelet fillings; luncheon soups, spreads, and salads; and the special brunch menus.

It *is* possible to prepare economical, nutritious breakfasts and lunches for 4 people in anywhere from 5 to 20 minutes using fresh ingredients. This chapter is filled with out-of-the-ordinary ideas that can revitalize everyone's interest in these two meals. You will find suggestions for meal-in-a-glass breakfast shakes, for sandwiches that can be eaten on the run, for making standard egg fare more exciting, and a way of preparing pancakes and French toast that makes them feasible weekday choices for the hurried cook.

Whether you pack a brown bag or lunchbox or eat at home, there are ways to add variety to routine lunches. Try the recipes for quick hot and cold soups that don't need to be simmered for hours. Or the ideas for perking up the common sandwich and those for "sandwiches" without bread. And, add the tasty salads and dressings to your lunch-away-from-home repertoire.

Simple purchased foods and insulated containers and bags make mix-on-the-spot meals and snacks possible. A carton of yogurt or cottage cheese and a container of cut-up fresh fruit or frozen berries can be mixed together at the office or at school for speedy nourishment. Whole fresh fruit or melon wedges, cheese, and crackers make a satisfying yet light breakfast or afternoon snack.

Use foods as natural coolers for lunches that must travel. Sandwiches without mayonnaise in the filling can be prepared ahead, frozen in individual bags, and added to the lunchbox straight from the

freezer. They will defrost by mealtime and will also keep other lunchbox items cool. The same approach can be used for cold soups.

Finally, for weekends when you and the family want something special — or for entertaining friends — there are 4 brunch menus that can be prepared in 30 minutes or less. Two are perfect for a luxurious late breakfast; the others are a true combination of breakfast and lunch. All let you enjoy weekend entertaining along with your guests.

Breakfast sandwiches are a great way to begin your day. Tasty, filling, and nutritious combinations such as this one (Tropical Ham, page 82) can be enjoyed at home or wrapped in foil to be eaten on the run.

Breakfast Shakes

Fast fruit shakes lend themselves to experimentation. The fruit shake chart shows the many options you have when in a hurry. Don't forget the "nutritious additions" for an energy boost. The amounts given are for 1 serving, but the measurements can easily be doubled. For 4 servings, blend in two batches. To get started, use the blended-drink recipes as guides. To prepare, simply blend or process all ingredients until smooth.

Preparation time: 5 to 8 minutes

With the nutritious additions, these energizing fruit shakes are a meal-in-a-glass (or commuter cup) and a super starter to your day.

Basic Fast Fruit Shake

- ½ cup sliced peaches
- ¼ cup orange, apple, *or* cranberry juice
- ¼ teaspoon cinnamon
- ¼ cup plain low-fat yogurt *or* skim milk
- ¼ teaspoon lemon juice
- ½ teaspoon brown sugar *or* honey
- 2 to 3 ice cubes

VARIATIONS
For the peaches substitute:
- ½ cup chopped cantaloupe.
- ½ cup drained mandarin orange segments.

Fruit Nog

- ¾ cup fruit of your choice
- 2 tablespoons frozen orange juice concentrate
- ¼ cup skim milk
- 1 tablespoon honey
- ¼ teaspoon vanilla
- 1 egg
- 2 to 3 ice cubes

Carob Shake

- ½ cup vanilla, carob, *or* coffee ice cream
- ½ banana, quartered
- 1 to 2 tablespoons dates and nuts of your choice
- 1½ tablespoons carob powder
- 1 egg

Orange-Banana Cream

- ½ cup *each* orange juice and vanilla ice cream *or* milk
- 1 tablespoon creamy *or* chunky peanut butter
- ½ small ripe banana, quartered
  Orange marmalade, to taste (for a sweeter shake)
- 3 ice cubes

Ingredients for Fast Fruit Shakes

Select 1 ingredient from each category, in the amount specified. Or, use 2 ingredients from the same category (such as peaches and pineapple), each in half the amount specified for that category. You can make a more fruity or creamy shake by omitting a category and increasing the proportions for the ingredients you prefer.

Fruits* (½ cup)	Dairy Products (¼ cup)	Juices (¼ cup)	Flavorings (¼ to ½ teaspoon or to taste)	Nutritious Additions (1 teaspoon)
Apples	Buttermilk	Apple	Brown sugar	Brewer's yeast
Apricots	Cottage cheese	Carrot	Cinnamon	Carob powder
Bananas	Cream cheese	Coconut	Coffee concentrate	High-protein powder
Blueberries	Egg, whole	Cranberry	Ginger	Nonfat dry milk
Cantaloupe	Ice cream, ice milk, or frozen yogurt	Grapefruit	Grape jelly	Nuts
Dates		Orange	Honey	Peanut butter
Honeydew melon	Milk: skim, whole, or nonfat dry	Papaya	Lemon juice	Sesame or sunflower seed
Kiwi fruit	Yogurt: plain or flavored	Pineapple	Nutmeg	Wheat germ
Mandarin oranges			Orange marmalade	
Papaya			Vanilla or almond extract	
Peaches				
Pineapple				
Strawberries				

*Use frozen or canned fruits when fresh are unavailable

Fruit Salads & Soups

Especially in the summer, fruit makes a refreshing breakfast. Here are a few out-of-the-ordinary ideas. Although one of the fruit soups must be chilled before serving, we've included it because it is unusual, easy to make, and very tasty. For a complete meal, add toast and your choice of beverage.

Preparation time: 10 to 20 minutes

Breakfast Salad

Combine 1 unpeeled, chopped apple, ⅓ cup *each* pumpkin *or* sunflower seeds and raisins, ¼ cup *each* chopped dates and dried apricots, and 1 sliced banana. Serve over cottage cheese *or* yogurt mixed with honey to taste. *Or*, serve in melon halves or as a topping for hot or cold whole-grain cereal.

Berry Soup

  1 tablespoon unflavored gelatin
  ¼ cup cold water
1¼ cups orange juice
  1 tablespoon lemon juice
  1 tablespoon kirsch (optional)
  1 pint *each* fresh *or* 1 package (10 oz) *each* frozen raspberries and strawberries
    Fresh mint leaves, for garnish

1. Soak gelatin in water.

2. Warm orange juice and dissolve gelatin in it.

3. Place in blender or food processor with remaining ingredients, blend, and chill.

4. Serve in glass bowls; garnish with mint leaves.

Variation: Substitute 2 pints fresh (or one 20-oz bag frozen) blueberries for the raspberries and strawberries.

Donna's Melon Soup

Halve and seed 2 cantaloupes *or* honeydew melons. Scoop out fruit (reserve shells) and purée in a blender (a little at a time) or a food processor. Season with a little lemon *or* lime juice and nutmeg *or* ginger. Spoon back into melon shells. Swirl a spoonful of sour cream into soup. Garnish with mint leaves.

VARIATIONS

Melon-Berry Soup

Add 1 cup strawberries, raspberries, *or* blueberries (with honeydew) to melon. Blend or process.

Peachy Melon Soup

Add half a 20-ounce bag frozen sliced peaches and 1 to 2 teaspoons almond *or* vanilla extract to melon. Blend or process.

Tropical Fruit Soup

Add 1 peeled, seeded, and chopped papaya and the grated peel of 1 orange and 1 lemon to cantaloupe. Blend or process. Garnish with chopped candied ginger.

Fresh Fruit Soup

Purée any chopped fresh fruit (peel if skin is tough) or whole berries in a blender or food processor. Thin to desired consistency by adding a complementary fruit juice *or* a few ice cubes. Sweeten with a little honey *or* sugar if desired.
  For variety, try one of the fruit combinations below.

- Pitted cherries (quick to do if you have a pitter) or plums thinned with pomegranate juice and flavored with almond *or* vanilla extract.

- Chopped mango, papaya, and pineapple thinned with lime juice and garnished with coconut and lime wheels.

- Berries puréed with kiwi fruit, peaches, nectarines, *or* bananas. Sweeten with a little mint, currant, *or* cranberry jelly and swirl a spoonful of plain yogurt *or* sour cream into the soup. Garnish with mint leaves and lemon wheels.

Fruit and Dip

Mix 2 cups chunky peanut butter with ½ cup sesame seed and ¼ teaspoon vanilla. Serve in small bowls to spread on sliced apples, pears, bananas, *or* firm peaches.

Colorful, unusual, and beautiful, fruit soups are a refreshing change from routine breakfast juices. Easily puréed in your blender, the soups can be made savory to sweet, depending on additions. With simple garnishes and served in glass bowls or melon shells, they are perfect for a festive Sunday brunch.

Breakfast Sandwiches

Try these sandwiches with juice or milk for a change of pace from eggs or cereal. Serve open-faced or topped with a second slice of toasted bread. Wrap in foil for out-of-hand eating or quarter the open-faced sandwiches. Many of these combinations are also good for lunch. Each recipe makes 4 sandwiches.

Preparation time: 15 minutes

Broiled Avocado Delight

Toast 4 slices whole grain bread. Layer 1 sliced avocado, 1 cup sliced fresh mushrooms, ⅓ cup toasted sliced almonds, and 4 slices tomato over the toast. Top each with a slice of any white cheese and broil until cheese melts.

Broiled Vegetarian

Sauté 1 cup sliced fresh mushrooms and ¼ cup *each* diced green *or* red pepper, onion, and zucchini just until softened. Distribute over 4 slices whole grain *or* rye toast. Top each with 1 slice white cheese and a sliced ripe olive. Broil until cheese melts.

Broiled Vegetarian with Egg

After broiling, top either of the preceding sandwiches with a fried egg. Serve open-faced.

Open-Faced Creamy Avocado

Peel, seed, and cut 2 avocados into chunks. Mix with ¼ to ½ cup sour cream, ricotta cheese, *or* yogurt. Mound on 4 slices whole grain *or* raisin toast. Sprinkle with sunflower seeds if desired.

Americana Favorite

Toast 8 slices raisin bread. Spread 4 with ½ cup plain *or* chunky peanut butter; the other 4 with 2 mashed bananas *or* ½ cup spiced apple butter. Distribute ¼ cup *each* raisins, shredded coconut, and sliced almonds over peanut butter. Top with toast spread with banana. Quarter for easy eating.

Tropical Ham

Top buttered raisin toast with 1 slice *each* baked ham, Swiss cheese, and pineapple. Sprinkle with cinnamon and nutmeg. Eat as is or broil to melt cheese.

BLT Breakfast

Mash 1 avocado with 2 tablespoons mayonnaise. Spread on 4 slices of toast. On each, layer 2 slices cooked bacon, 2 slices tomato, and a butter lettuce leaf *or* a handful of alfalfa sprouts. Top with second slice of toast and quarter for easy eating.

Variation: Add sliced cheese, sautéed chopped mushrooms, and chopped peppers *or* chiles.

Sausage

Sauté ½ pound hot *or* mild Italian sausage, crumbled, until browned (3 to 5 minutes). Drain off all fat. Add ¼ cup tomato sauce, 1 chopped green pepper, half a chopped small red onion, ½ teaspoon *each* oregano and basil, and 6 to 8 beaten eggs. Cook, stirring, until eggs are set. Serve in halved pita bread.

Variation: Substitute ½ cup shredded Monterey jack *or* mozzarella cheese for the tomato sauce.

Croissant

Sprinkle 4 croissants with a few drops of water and heat in a 350°F oven. Fill with one of the following:

- Omelet seasoned with herb of your choice. (See page 85.)
- Slices of ham, cheese, and pineapple.
- Cream cheese and a slice of smoked salmon (lox).

Quesadillas

Preheat oven to 450°F. Cover the right-hand half of 4 large flour tortillas with a mixture of shredded Cheddar and Monterey jack cheese (¾ cup *each*). Top each with 1 tablespoon canned diced green chiles and a dollop of salsa (optional). You can also add sliced green *or* red onions and diced avocado. Fold tortillas in half; press to seal. Place on baking sheet and bake until cheese melts and tortillas are golden (5 minutes). If not eating out of hand, top with sour cream after baking.

Variation: Fill tortillas with ¾ cup grated cheese and ¾ cup diced cooked bacon, ham, sausage, chicken, turkey, *or* beef. Seal and bake as directed.

When you're on the run, make a quick, nutritious sandwich, pop it in the toaster oven, wrap in foil, and take it with you.

Good Food

Food that is good for you and easy to put together — use basic ingredients to make nutritious breakfast sandwich combinations as an alternative to sweets. They can be eaten out of hand or with a knife and fork. Try them with your kids for a welcome breakfast change.

Egg in a Hole

Using a round cookie cutter or the rim of a small glass, cut a circle from the center of each of 4 slices of bread. (Cut-out center may be browned in the same pan or in a toaster and served alongside.)

Melt 2 tablespoons butter in a large frying pan; add bread. Crack an egg into each hole. Cook until eggs are set. Lift bread with a spatula and add 2 more tablespoons butter to pan. Flip bread over carefully, to cook second side. Season with salt and pepper before serving.

Egg Salad in Pita Halves

Chop 6 to 8 hard-cooked eggs and mix with ¼ cup mayonnaise and about 1 cup canned salmon (or other seafood). Spoon into halved pita bread and garnish with watercress leaves.

Poultry-Citrus Eye-Opener

Spread 4 slices of raisin or rye toast with spiced apple butter. Top each with sliced turkey and orange or grapefruit segments, sliced nectarines, or canned mandarin orange segments.

Cheese and Fruit

Spread 4 slices of bread with cottage cheese (plain or mixed with pineapple). Top with orange segments, pineapple chunks, or banana slices and sprinkle with nuts or wheat germ. Drizzle honey over top.

French Toast, Pancakes, & Toppings

No need to stand over a hot griddle when making French toast or pancakes. With this no-fuss oven-baking approach, both can join the ranks of Monday-through-Friday breakfast fare for 4. Make one of the luscious flavored toppings while breakfast bakes.

Preparation time: 15 minutes

Oven-Baked French Toast

    4 eggs
    1 tablespoon sugar
1½ cups milk
    ¼ teaspoon nutmeg
    ½ teaspoon salt
    8 to 10 slices day-old bread

1. Preheat oven to 475°F. Generously butter 2 large baking sheets.

2. In blender or food processor, combine all ingredients (except bread). Pour mixture into a shallow dish. Dip bread into egg mixture, allowing each slice to absorb as much liquid as possible.

3. Arrange slices on baking sheets and bake 5 minutes per side or until golden.

4. Dust with powdered sugar, cut in half diagonally, and serve with jelly, syrup, or sour cream.

Oven-Baked Wheat Pancakes

For added nutritional value, substitute buckwheat, barley, oatmeal, or soy flour or wheat germ for ¼ cup of the whole wheat flour. The recipe makes 1 dozen pancakes.

    2 cups buttermilk, sour milk, *or* orange juice
    2 eggs
    1 tablespoon brown sugar *or* honey
    2 cups whole wheat flour
    1 teaspoon baking soda
½ teaspoon salt
    1 tablespoon melted butter

1. Preheat oven to 450°F. Generously butter 2 large baking sheets and place in oven.

2. Combine all ingredients. Do not overmix. Batter should be lumpy.

3. Ladle pancakes onto hot baking sheets and bake 10 minutes. You do *not* need to turn pancakes.

Zestier Syrups

Orange: To 2 cups purchased syrup, add ⅓ cup orange juice *or* ¼ cup Cointreau and grated peel of half an orange.

Gingered: To 2 cups purchased syrup, add ⅓ cup orange juice and 1 tablespoon finely grated fresh *or* 1 teaspoon ground ginger.

Lemon: To 2 cups purchased syrup, add lemon juice to taste (start with 2 tablespoons) and grated peel of half a lemon.

A quick-and-easy whole wheat batter, zesty toppings, and flavored butters turn a familiar pancake breakfast into something truly special.

Flavored Whipped Cream

Maple: Whip ½ pint (1 cup) cream and fold in 1 tablespoon maple syrup.

Citrus: Whip ½ pint (1 cup) cream and fold in 2 teaspoons grated lime *or* lemon peel, a little lime *or* lemon juice, and powdered sugar to taste. This cream is wonderful on whole strawberries and on papaya or pineapple slices.

Flavored Sour Cream or Ricotta

Honeyed: Mix ½ cup *each* sour cream *or* ricotta cheese and plain yogurt. Add 1 tablespoon honey and grated peel and juice of 1 lime or lemon *or* half an orange.

Fruited: Mix ½ cup *each* sour cream *or* ricotta cheese and plain yogurt. Add 1 tablespoon favorite jelly, jam, *or* preserves.

Flavored Butters

Flavored butters are especially attractive when rolled into balls or formed in molds. They may be made in quantity and frozen. Thaw before serving.

Autumn: Beat ¼ to ⅓ cup firmly packed brown sugar *or* honey, 1 teaspoon pumpkin pie spice, and ¼ to ½ cup whipping cream into 1 cup (2 cubes) softened butter *or* margarine.

Fruit-Nut: Beat ⅓ cup finely chopped dried dates, prunes, *or* apricots and 1 cup ground walnuts *or* pecans into 1 cup (2 cubes) softened butter *or* margarine.

Honey-Nut: Beat ⅓ to ½ cup honey and 2 tablespoons ground macadamia nuts, hazelnuts, *or* almonds into 1 cup (2 cubes) softened butter *or* margarine.

Omelets

Omelets take only a bit more time to make than scrambled eggs, but seem more special. The technique is simple, and the possibilities for fillings practically unlimited. Allow 3 to 4 tablespoons of filling for each single-serving omelet.

Preparation time: 15 to 20 minutes for 4 single-serving omelets

Basic Single-Serving Omelet with Herbs

3 eggs
1 tablespoon water
2 tablespoons butter
1 teaspoon *each* minced fresh parsley, tarragon, and chives

1. Preheat a 7 or 8-inch omelet pan over medium-high heat.

2. Mix eggs and water with a fork until well blended but not foamy.

3. Add butter to skillet; when it foams, pour in the eggs. Slowly stir counterclockwise 3 times with a fork. Allow eggs to cook for a few seconds. Then draw eggs toward center of skillet, creating a fan effect.

4. Add herbs (or a filling of your choice) and fold omelet in half with spatula. Shake pan gently, tilt over warmed serving plate, and slide omelet out. Or, quickly invert with a flick of your wrist.

Once you master the omelet technique, filling variations are limitless. Or filled with a sweet, an omelet also makes a tasty dessert.

FILLING VARIATIONS

Spicy Spanish
Add ¼ cup of the following mixture in Step 4: diced green (mild) or jalapeño (hot) chiles, black olives, and any shredded cheese. Top with a dash of salsa *or* a dollop of sour cream or yogurt to cool the spiciness.

Apple-Roquefort
Sauté half a tart green apple, cored and thinly sliced, in 1 tablespoon butter. In Step 4, add apple, grated Parmesan *or* shredded Monterey jack cheese, and ½ to 1 ounce Roquefort cheese. Garnish with watercress leaves.

Spinach
Add ¼ cup sautéed chopped fresh spinach, 1 diced anchovy fillet, 1 tablespoon shredded cheese, and a sprinkling of grated Parmesan cheese to omelet in Step 4. Garnish omelet with a fresh spinach leaf.

Provençal
Sauté ¼ cup diced tomatoes in olive oil and garlic. Add to omelet in Step 4. Sprinkle omelet with minced fresh parsley before serving.

Princess
Add ¼ cup cooked asparagus tips mixed with a little whipping cream in Step 4. Garnish with sliced, raw mushrooms and cooked asparagus tips.

Creole
Add 1 tablespoon *each* diced tomato, onion, pimiento, and parsley plus ½ minced clove garlic to eggs before adding to pan. Fill omelet with 2 tablespoons sautéed sliced okra (optional) *or* shredded sharp Cheddar cheese.

Lorraine
Add 2 tablespoons *each* cooked diced bacon and shredded Gruyère or any white cheese, and a little chopped green onion in Step 4.

Garden Patch
Add ¼ cup sautéed or steamed diced mixed vegetables (leftovers are fine) in Step 4.

Artichoke
Add ¼ cup (total) diced ham, drained chopped artichoke hearts, and shredded Muenster cheese in Step 4.

Hearty
Add 2 tablespoons *each* sautéed sliced chicken livers and sliced mushrooms in Step 4. Top with a dollop of sour cream and a sliced ripe olive.

Italian
Add 3 tablespoons cooked crumbled Italian sausage and 1 teaspoon chopped fresh (or ¼ teaspoon dried) basil to omelet in Step 4. Sprinkle omelet with grated Parmesan, Romano, or Fontina cheese before serving.

Smoked Salmon
Add 1 slice smoked salmon (lox), cut into strips; 2 tablespoons crumbled cream cheese; and a sprinkling of lemon juice to omelet in Step 4. Sprinkle omelet with chopped chives before serving.

Luncheon Soups

Hot or cold soups, with a roll and salad or some fruit, make a complete and nutritious lunch. Lightweight, nonbreakable plastic containers that keep foods hot or cold — as well as the traditional thermos — also make it possible for soups to be the main course for lunch away from home. As these recipes prove, soups need not be simmered for hours. They can be prepared in 8 to 20 minutes using a food processor or a blender. All serve 4 people.

Cold Cream of Avocado Soup

- 1 large, ripe avocado, peeled, seeded, and roughly chopped
  Half a medium onion, roughly chopped
- 3 tablespoons plain yogurt
- 3 to 4 dashes Worcestershire sauce or dry sherry
- ⅛ teaspoon white pepper
- 1½ cups chicken broth, chilled
- ½ cup whipping cream or buttermilk
  Chopped chives or chervil, for garnish

In a blender or food processor, whirl all ingredients (except chives) until smooth. Serve immediately or chill. Garnish with chives before serving.

Preparation time: 8 minutes

Variation: Add 1 clove garlic before processing. Stir in 1 can (6 oz) drained shrimp or clams before serving.

Cold Cream of Normandy Soup

- 1 large red onion, sliced
- 1 apple, unpeeled, cored, and sliced
- 1 tablespoon butter
- 1 tablespoon curry powder
- ¼ cup flour
- 2 cans (14½ oz *each*) chicken broth
- 1 cup whipping cream
- 2 egg yolks
  Salt, pepper, and lemon juice to taste
- 1 apple, unpeeled, cored, and diced
  Watercress sprigs, for garnish

1. In a large saucepan over low to medium heat, cook onion and apple in butter just until tender (about 5 minutes). Pan should be covered.

2. Add curry powder and flour and cook until bubbly.

3. Add broth and bring to a boil. Reduce heat and simmer 5 minutes.

4. Mix cream and egg yolks. Stir a little hot soup into the cream-yolk mixture, and add it to the hot soup. Simmer until thickened. Do not boil or egg yolk will curdle.

5. Process or blend soup until smooth. Season and chill.

6. Before serving, add diced apple. Garnish with watercress.

Preparation time: 20 to 25 minutes

Blender Borsch

If you start with cold beets and broth, this soup will not need to be chilled further before serving.

- 1 can (16 oz) sliced beets, drained
- 1 can (14½ oz) chicken broth
- ¼ cup roughly chopped onion
- 1 clove garlic
- 1 tablespoon lemon juice
- 2 teaspoons sugar
- ½ cup sour cream or plain yogurt
- 1 cucumber, peeled and coarsely chopped (optional)
- 1 tablespoon fresh or ½ teaspoon dried dill or fennel
  Sliced hard-cooked egg, for garnish

1. Combine first 6 ingredients in blender or processor. Whirl until thoroughly mixed.

2. Stir in sour cream, cucumber, and dill. Garnish with slices of egg.

Preparation time: 8 minutes

Corn and Cheddar Cheese Chowder

- 1 medium onion, chopped
- ½ cup sliced celery
- 2 tablespoons butter
- ¼ cup flour
- 1 quart milk (at room temperature)
- 1 can (16 oz) cream-style or whole-kernel corn
- 1 can (16 oz) diced or sliced potatoes
- ½ to 1 cup shredded sharp Cheddar cheese
  Salt, pepper, and paprika to taste
- 2 strips bacon, cooked and crumbled, for garnish

1. In a large kettle, sauté onion and celery in butter just until tender (about 5 minutes).

2. Blend in flour and cook until bubbly. Add milk and bring to a boil, stirring occasionally until thickened.

3. Add remaining ingredients and heat through (5 minutes). Season. Garnish with crumbled bacon before serving.

Preparation time: 15 minutes

Seafood Tureen

- 1 tablespoon butter
- 1 pound mixed fish fillets (red snapper, sea bass, cod, sole, or salmon), cut in chunks
- 1½ cups dry white wine
- 1 cup cooked small shrimp
- 1 cup lobster meat (optional, but if omitted, add 1 cup other fish)
- ¼ pound (10 medium) mushrooms, sliced
- 1 can (16 oz) whole tomatoes and juice (break up tomatoes) or 1 can (14½ oz) chicken broth
- 1 to 2 cloves garlic, minced
- ⅛ teaspoon saffron or ¼ teaspoon turmeric
- ¼ to ½ cup dry sherry (optional)
  Salt and pepper to taste

1. Melt butter in a large kettle. Add fish fillets and wine. Cover and simmer just until fish becomes opaque (5 to 8 minutes).

2. Add remaining ingredients (except sherry) and simmer 5 minutes.

3. Stir in sherry if desired. Season.

Preparation time: 15 minutes

Variation: Add ¼ to ½ cup *each* diced celery and carrot with the fish fillets.

This low-calorie cream soup base contains no cream — nonfat dry milk helps thicken the roux. When the milk base is made, add any puréed vegetable for both color and nutrition. For a finishing touch, stir 1 tablespoon of Champagne or sherry into each serving.

Cream of Any Vegetable Soup

This cream soup base is low in cost, calories, and cholesterol. Add your favorite vegetable or combination, or try one of our ideas. The soup can be served hot or chilled.

　1　medium onion, thinly sliced *or* 1 bunch green onions, sliced
　4　tablespoons butter
　2　tablespoons *each* flour and non-instant, nonfat dry milk
　4　cups whole milk, at room temperature

1. Sauté onion in butter until softened.

2. Stir in flour and dry milk and cook until bubbly.

3. Gradually add whole milk, stirring until soup is smooth. Heat, stirring occasionally, until soup thickens.

4. Add your choice of vegetable. (See Variations.)

5. Process or blend soup until smooth. Serve hot or chill.

Preparation time: 20 to 25 minutes

VARIATIONS

Cream of Lettuce
Add 3 to 4 cups shredded iceberg lettuce to soup in Step 4. Cook, covered, for 3 minutes. After processing, stir in dry sherry to taste (optional). Sprinkle with paprika or nutmeg.

Cream of Mushroom
Replace 2 cups of the whole milk in the basic recipe with 1 can (14½ oz) chicken *or* beef broth. In Step 4, add 1 pound (40 medium) sliced *or* chopped mushrooms and ¼ cup chopped fresh parsley. Cook, covered, until mushrooms are soft (about 5 minutes). After processing, stir in 1 cup plain yogurt *or* sour cream. Sprinkle with nutmeg or mace.

Cream of Watercress
Remove stalks from 3 bunches watercress. Add to soup in Step 4. Cook, covered, for 3 minutes. After processing, garnish each serving with a dash of nutmeg and a slice of lemon.

Cream of Spinach
Remove stems from 2 bunches fresh spinach and roughly chop leaves. (Or, thaw two 10-ounce packages frozen chopped spinach.) Add to soup in Step 4 and simmer 3 minutes. After processing, season with ¼ teaspoon thyme and stir in 1 cup plain yogurt. Garnish with sieved egg yolk.

Cream of Carrot
Scrub and slice 8 to 10 carrots. Add to soup in Step 3 and simmer until tender (10 to 12 minutes). After processing, stir in 1 to 2 teaspoons dillweed.

Cream of Asparagus
Roughly chop 1 pound of asparagus (tough portion of stems removed). Add asparagus and ½ cup chopped celery to soup in Step 4 and simmer until tender (5 to 7 minutes). After processing, add dry sherry to taste (optional).

Cream of Broccoli
Roughly chop 1 pound of broccoli. Add to soup in Step 4 and simmer until tender (6 to 8 minutes). After processing, add dry sherry to taste (optional).

Cream of Cauliflower
Roughly chop 1 medium head cauliflower. Add to soup in Step 4 and simmer until just tender (10 minutes). After processing, stir in ½ cup shredded Cheddar cheese.

Sandwich Ideas

Alleviate lunchtime boredom with a bit of imagination. To make the standard sandwich more appealing, combine fillings and condiments in new ways, substitute other greens or sprouts for lettuce, and use a variety of breads and rolls — or make a sandwich without bread. With vegetable sticks, fruit, and one of the No-Bake Cookies (page 74), a sandwich makes a hearty and satisfying mid-day meal.

Preparation time: 10 to 15 minutes

Homemade Nut Butters

For a change from peanut butter, make your own nut butters. They're quick and easy to prepare in a blender or food processor. Use salted or unsalted almonds, cashews, walnuts, or pecans — or combine types. For each cup of nuts, add 1 to 3 tablespoons salad oil while processing. Try one of the sandwich combinations below.

- Nut butter, honey, and sliced mango or papaya.
- Nut butter, honey, and bananas or coconut.
- Nut butter, spiced apple butter, and diced or grated apple.
- Nut butter, spiced apple butter, and trail mix.
- Nut butter, applesauce, wheat germ, and raisins.
- Nut butter, honey, and crumbled cooked bacon.

Stuffed Sandwiches

Fill hollowed-out French rolls or halved pita bread with any of these fillings.

- Curried Tuna and Fruit Salad (page 90).
- Nutted Chicken or Turkey Salad or a variation (page 90).
- Diced cooked sausage, chopped mushrooms, and diced celery mixed with mayonnaise, mustard, and chutney.
- Ratatouille (cooked vegetables in tomato sauce).
- Guacamole (avocado mashed with lemon juice, onion, and a little hot salsa), sliced banana, pineapple, and spinach leaves.
- Guacamole, sliced tomato, onion, olives, and spinach or lettuce leaves.
- Equal parts ground ham and crushed pineapple mixed with mayonnaise and Dijon-style mustard to taste.
- Deviled ham seasoned with horseradish and a few capers.
- Braunschweiger sausage, tomato paste, and a few drops Worcestershire sauce blended until smooth.
- Equal parts shredded Swiss or Monterey jack cheese and chopped walnuts, diced carrot and celery, and mayonnaise and mustard to taste.

Roll-Up Sandwiches

Sandwiches don't necessarily have to include bread. Try some of these ideas. All should be secured with a toothpick after rolling.

- Wrap any sandwich filling in a lettuce or cabbage leaf.
- Roll beef, ham, or turkey around a dill or sweet pickle spear.
- Roll sliced cheese around a carrot or celery stick.
- Spread one side of a bologna slice with Cheddar cheese spread. Roll, with cheese inside.

Twelve noon does not have to mean a tuna or peanut butter-and-jelly sandwich on the same old bread. Try new breads, as well as spreads and fillings like the ones shown here. From left to right: nut-mushroom paté, carrot-cauliflower paté, homemade cashew-walnut butter, and sugar pea-sesame spread. Also use the spreads as dips for familiar vegetables—raw green beans, asparagus, broccoli, cauliflower, snow or edible-pod peas, cherry tomatoes, and whole mushrooms—and not-so-familiar vegetables—sliced raw turnips, jicama, Jerusalem artichokes, and kohlrabi.

Patés & Spreads

For those who like a light lunch, or as an accompaniment for soup or a meat or seafood salad, these vegetable mixtures can't be beat. Serve them as dips for raw vegetable slices, sticks, or flowerets or as spreads for crackers or bread. They also make tasty vegetarian sandwich fillings.

Preparation time: 15 to 20 minutes

Sugar Pea-Sesame Spread

    ¼ cup sesame seed
    2 tablespoons butter
    1 onion, thinly sliced
    1 to 2 cloves garlic, minced
   10 ounces fresh or 1 package (10 oz) frozen sugar peas, thawed
    ¼ cup dry sherry
    2 teaspoons lemon juice
      Salt and pepper to taste

1. Toast sesame seed in a skillet, over medium heat, shaking frequently (about 5 minutes). Remove from pan.

2. Add butter and sauté onion and garlic until onion is limp. Add peas, sherry, and lemon juice and cook until barely tender (about 5 minutes).

3. Process or blend until smooth. Add sesame seed; season.

Nut-Mushroom Paté

    1 package (10 oz) whole blanched almonds
    1 teaspoon butter
    1 small onion, quartered
    1 to 2 cloves garlic, peeled
    ¾ pound (30 medium) mushrooms, halved
    1 tablespoon butter
    ½ teaspoon salt
    ¼ teaspoon dried thyme or tarragon
    ¼ cup yogurt or sour cream
    1 to 2 tablespoons dry sherry (optional)

1. In a skillet, toast almonds in the 1 teaspoon butter, shaking pan occasionally (about 5 minutes).

2. Meanwhile, process or blend onion and garlic with short on-off bursts until coarsely chopped. Remove from container and process or blend mushrooms in the same way.

3. Melt the 1 tablespoon butter and add onions, garlic, mushrooms, and seasonings. Cook over medium-high heat, shaking pan occasionally, until most of the liquid has evaporated.

4. Reserving ½ cup of the almonds, process or blend the remainder until finely ground.

5. Add vegetables (with remaining liquid) and sour cream to container with nuts and process until almost smooth. Add sherry to taste.

6. Place in a bowl or terrine, garnish with reserved almonds, cover, and chill.

Carrot-Cauliflower Paté

    1 tablespoon butter
    1 small onion, sliced
    1 to 2 cloves garlic, minced
    1 cup each thinly sliced carrot and cauliflower
    ½ teaspoon each curry powder and salt
    ⅔ cup water
    1 cup salted cashews or peanuts
   1½ to 2 tablespoons oil

1. Melt butter and sauté onion and garlic until soft. Add carrot, cauliflower, curry powder, and salt and sauté briefly.

2. Add water, cover skillet, and bring liquid to a boil. Reduce heat and simmer 6 to 8 minutes.

3. Meanwhile, in a blender or processor, finely grind ¾ cup of the nuts. Gradually add oil, processing continuously until mixture is creamy and smooth.

4. Add vegetables and process until smooth. Stir in the remaining ¼ cup nuts.

5. Serve at room temperature or chill.

Salads & Dressings

Whether a mixture of greens and chopped vegetables or a more substantial combination that includes meat or seafood, salads are lunchtime favorites. They are also a perfect way to make use of small amounts of leftovers. Add cooked vegetables marinated in a little vinegar and oil, sliced or wedged hard-cooked eggs, flaked fish or chopped meat, fresh or canned fruit, and sliced or diced cheeses of all kinds. With bread or a roll and perhaps a light soup, you have a filling meal.

Salads make good box or bag lunches as long as you pack the dressing separately from the greens and the meat or fish mixture. Insulated plastic containers will keep everything cool until lunchtime.

We've given recipes for two quick but special meat and seafood salads. Both can also be used as sandwich fillings. We've also included an unusual fruit salad and dip and a selection of salad dressings. All recipes serve 4. For many other salad ideas, refer to Ortho's *The Complete Book of Salads*.

Preparation time: 5 to 15 minutes

Nutted Chicken or Turkey Salad

- 1½ to 2 cups diced or shredded cooked chicken *or* turkey
- ½ cup sliced celery
- ¼ cup *each* chopped green onion and salted almonds
- 2 teaspoons *each* lemon juice and Dijon-style mustard
- ¼ teaspoon salt
- ¼ cup *each* mayonnaise and yogurt

Combine all ingredients.

VARIATIONS

Spicy

Substitute ¼ to ½ cup French dressing for the mayonnaise and yogurt. Garnish with sliced pimiento, olives, hard-cooked eggs, and capers.

Or, substitute walnuts for the almonds and garnish with cucumber slices.

Fruited

For the mayonnaise and yogurt, substitute ¼ cup *each* sour cream and mayonnaise and 1 teaspoon *each* sugar and lemon juice. Add about ½ cup diced apples, halved grapes, pineapple chunks, *or* orange segments (fresh or canned) to the salad.

Oriental

To the 1½ to 2 cups chicken or turkey, add ½ cup sliced water chestnuts and ½ cup bean sprouts. Mix with ¼ cup *each* mayonnaise and yogurt. Season with salt, sugar, and ground coriander (start with ¼ teaspoon) to taste.

Curried Tuna and Fruit Salad

- ¼ cup *each* mayonnaise and plain yogurt
- 2 tablespoons lemon juice
- 1 to 2 teaspoons curry powder
- 1 tablespoon chutney, chopped
- 2 cans (6½ oz *each*) chunk-style tuna, drained
- 1 cup thinly sliced celery
- ¼ cup thinly sliced green onion
- 2 apples, cored and diced
- 1 cup seedless grapes *or* raisins
  Shredded coconut and almonds, for garnish

Combine first 5 ingredients thoroughly. Gently mix in remaining ingredients. Garnish.

Summer Salad

- 4 sliced peaches
- 2 sliced pears (dipped in lemon juice)
  Half a pineapple, cut in chunks
- 1 pint fresh strawberries
- 12 broccoli flowerets
- 12 cooked medium-size shrimp
- 8 slices baked *or* boiled ham, rolled
  Lettuce leaves
  Watercress Mayonnaise Dip (recipe follows)

1. Arrange fruits, vegetables, shrimp, and ham on lettuce leaves.

2. Serve with Watercress Mayonnaise Dip (in individual bowls). Provide toothpicks or seafood forks for dipping.

Watercress Mayonnaise Dip

- 1 bunch watercress sprigs, roughly chopped
- 3 tablespoons lemon juice
- ¼ teaspoon tarragon
- 1 clove garlic, minced
- 1 cup mayonnaise

Combine all ingredients in a blender or food processor. Process until smooth.

Mustard Vinaigrette Dressing

This dressing is delicious on or mixed with green, meat, or bean salads. Vary the flavor by adding a minced fresh herb (or herbs) of your choice and by using flavored vinegars and olive or nut oil.

- 1 teaspoon *each* salt and Dijon-style mustard
- ¼ teaspoon freshly ground black pepper
- 1 clove garlic, crushed
- ¼ cup red wine vinegar
- 2 tablespoons lemon juice
- ⅔ cup salad oil

Mix first 5 ingredients in a small bowl (or a screw-top jar) to allow the vinegar to dissolve the salt. Whisk in lemon juice and oil (or cap jar and shake vigorously).

VARIATIONS

Egg Vinaigrette

Whisk in yolk of a soft-boiled egg with the lemon juice; then whisk in oil. Add chopped egg white to finished dressing.

Hearty Vinaigrette

Add one or a combination of the following to the basic Mustard Vinaigrette: minced shallots, chives, pimiento, or anchovy fillets; chopped cornichons or gherkins; capers.

This Summer Salad with its tangy Watercress Mayonnaise Dip makes a delicious finger-food lunch. Serve it with croissants or muffins.

Spicy Avocado Dressing

This dressing goes well with green or citrus-and-green salads, and it makes a tasty substitute for mayonnaise in chicken or turkey salads.

- 1 cup plain yogurt *or* mayonnaise
- 1 ripe avocado, peeled, seeded, and roughly chopped
- ⅓ cup lemon juice
- 2 tablespoons milk
- ½ teaspoon salt
- 1 clove garlic, crushed
- ¼ teaspoon *each* hot pepper sauce and cumin

In a blender or food processor, blend all ingredients until thoroughly combined.

Lemon-Lime Yogurt Dressing

This tangy dressing is great on meat or fish salads. Flavor it with Dijon-style mustard for meat and with dill for fish salads.

- 2 cups plain yogurt
- ¼ cup *each* lemon and lime juice
- 3 hard-cooked egg yolks
- 6 shallots, peeled *or* ¼ cup roughly chopped green or red onion
- ⅓ cup chopped fresh parsley
  Salt and freshly ground pepper to taste
- 3 hard-cooked egg whites, chopped (optional)

In a blender or food processor, blend all ingredients (except egg whites) until thoroughly combined. Stir in chopped whites if desired.

Citrus-Honey Dressing

This is a tasty sweet dressing for fruit salads, or for green or meat salads that contain fruit.

- 1 cup *each* ricotta *or* cottage cheese and plain yogurt
- 2 tablespoons honey
- 2 tablespoons chopped fresh mint
  Grated peel of 1 lemon and 1 lime
- 1 tablespoon *each* lemon and lime juice

In a blender or food processor, blend all ingredients until thoroughly combined.

VARIATIONS

Orangerie Dressing

Substitute the grated peel and juice of 1 orange for the lime.

Poppy Seed Dressing

Omit the mint. Add 1 to 2 tablespoons poppy seed to dressing after blending.

Gingered Fruit Dressing

Substitute ½ teaspoon ground ginger *or* 1 teaspoon grated fresh ginger root *or* 1 tablespoon chopped candied ginger for the mint.

Almond Dressing

Omit the mint. Mix ½ cup ground almonds *or* filberts with 1 to 2 tablespoons sherry *or* orange juice to make a paste. Blend with remaining ingredients.

Brunch Menus

Macadamia-Banana French Toast

Bacon or Sausage

Fresh Orange-Grapefruit Juice

Beverage suggestion:
Hawaiian Coconut Extravaganza
or Sparkling Gamay Beaujolais

Macadamia-Banana French Toast

This idea comes from a small restaurant on Maui, where fruits and nuts are served on top of waffles and French toast.

- 1 banana, quartered
- 4 eggs
- 1 jar (3½ oz) Macadamia nuts, crushed *or* processed and divided into 2 equal portions (reserve a few whole nuts for garnish)
- 1 cup milk
- 1 teaspoon vanilla
    Dash cinnamon *or* nutmeg
- 8 to 10 slices day-old whole wheat *or* white bread
    Powdered sugar
- 2 bananas, sliced

1. Preheat oven to 475°F. Generously butter 2 large baking sheets.

2. In a blender or food processor, whirl the banana, eggs, half the crushed nuts, milk, vanilla, and cinnamon until well mixed. (Or, beat with an electric mixer.)

3. Halve bread slices diagonally and arrange in a large, shallow dish. Pour egg mixture over bread, allow bread to absorb egg, then turn and coat other side.

4. Arrange slices on baking sheets. Bake 5 minutes per side or until golden.

5. Remove from baking sheets and dust with powdered sugar. Top with banana slices, half the crushed nuts, and reserved whole nuts.

VARIATIONS

Pineapple-Coconut French Toast

Drain juice from 1 can (8 oz) crushed pineapple and add juice to egg batter in place of banana. Follow basic recipe. Top French toast with pineapple and with ½ cup shredded coconut.

Papaya French Toast

Follow basic recipe, but do not add banana to egg batter. Top French toast with 1 sliced papaya and a dollop of whipped or sour cream *or* one of the flavored creams (page 84).

This menu will please the most discriminating palate. Blending a banana with the egg batter produces a moist, richly flavored French toast, and the oven-baking technique makes preparation a snap. When you're selecting brunch menus to try, don't pass up this one.

Bacon or Sausage

Fry about ½ pound (8 to 12 slices or links) bacon or sausage until crisp.

Fresh Orange-Grapefruit Juice

- 1½ cups freshly squeezed orange juice
- ½ cup freshly squeezed grapefruit juice
    Mint sprigs, for garnish

Combine juices and chill. Garnish with mint sprigs before serving.

Hawaiian Coconut Extravaganza

This refreshing drink is a striking accompaniment to the French toast. Time for its preparation is *not* included within the 30-minute cooking plan.

- 4 coconuts
- 4 generous jiggers rum
- 4 tablespoons *each* Cointreau and coconut cream *or* CocoRibe
- 3 cups crushed ice

1. Saw off (and reserve) the tops of the coconuts. (The hole should be about 1 inch in diameter.)

2. Add ¼ of each remaining ingredient to each coconut.

3. Cover holes with reserved tops and shake to mix. Provide straws for sipping.

COOKING PLAN

1. Assemble all ingredients and cooking equipment.

2. Prepare fruit juice and chill.

3. Preheat oven to 475°F. Butter baking sheets. Grind nuts.

4. Prepare egg batter for French toast. Halve bread slices and coat with batter.

5. Place French toast in oven. Fry bacon or sausage.

6. Slice fruit for French toast.

To serve: Garnish fruit juice with mint. Remove French toast from oven and top with sugar, fruit, and nuts. Drain bacon or sausage and serve.

2

German Puffed Apple Pancake

Canadian Bacon

Beverage suggestion:
Hot spiced cider with cinnamon stick

German Puffed Apple Pancake

This pancake — also called Dutch baby or
Pfannküchen — makes an impressive dessert as well. Prepare it in a heavy 12-inch
ovenproof skillet or round baking dish no
more than 3 inches deep.

Pancake:
  2 tablespoons butter
  3 eggs
  ¾ cup *each* milk and flour
  ¼ to ½ teaspoon salt

Topping:
  2 tablespoons butter
  1 pound tart apples, cored and thinly
    sliced
  3 to 4 tablespoons sugar
  ⅛ teaspoon *each* ground cinnamon
    and nutmeg

Garnishes:
  Powdered sugar and lemon wedges

While you prepare other menu items, this pancake puffs in your oven. It also makes a dramatic
dessert when topped with Cognac and served aflame. Accompany it with bacon or sausages.

1. To prepare pancake, melt butter in an
ovenproof skillet in 450°F oven.

2. In a blender or food processor, mix
remaining pancake ingredients until
smooth, adding one by one.

3. Pour batter into skillet, return to oven,
and bake 15 minutes. As pancake cooks,
it will puff and large bubbles may form.
Check periodically and pierce bubbles
with a fork or toothpick.

4. To prepare topping, melt butter and
sauté apples over medium-high heat.
Add sugar and spices; stir. Cook until
tender-crisp (6 to 8 minutes).

5. When pancake is done, remove from
oven and spoon topping into center.
Sprinkle with powdered sugar.

6. Slice pancake into wedges and serve
at once, garnished with lemon wedges.

VARIATIONS

■ For the apples, substitute any seasonal
fresh fruit or a combination. Banana
and papaya slices, with lime rather
than lemon wedges, are very tasty.

■ For the apples, substitute canned pie
filling flavored with lemon juice and
ground cinnamon to taste.

■ Top warm or cold pancake with sour
cream *or* plain yogurt and a little orange marmalade. Or, simply top pancake with honey *or* maple syrup.

Canadian Bacon

Wrap 8 slices Canadian bacon in aluminum foil. Seal securely. Warm in oven
while pancake bakes (5 to 10 minutes).

C O O K I N G   P L A N

1. Assemble all ingredients and cooking
equipment.

2. Slice apples. Wrap Canadian bacon
in foil.

3. Melt butter for pancake in 450°F oven.
Prepare pancake batter and bake.

4. Prepare apple topping. Place
Canadian bacon in oven.

5. Cut lemon into wedges.

To serve: Remove pancake from oven,
top with apples, and garnish. Serve with
Canadian bacon.

3 Individual Cheese Soufflés en Surprise

Lemon-Butter Asparagus

Fresh Fruit Platter

Croissants

Wine suggestion:
Chardonnay

Individual Cheese Soufflés en Surprise

With their tasty filling, these individual soufflés are elegant brunch offerings. Substitute other grated cheeses or herbs for a different flavor twist. Ricotta acts as a low-calorie binder for the ingredients, eliminating the typical white-sauce soufflé base.

Filling:

- 1 teaspoon butter
- ½ cup chopped fresh mushrooms
- 2 to 3 tablespoons minced green *or* red onion
- 1 tablespoon minced fresh parsley
- ¼ teaspoon *each* dried basil and thyme

Soufflé:

- 6 eggs, separated
- 2 tablespoons Cognac *or* brandy
- ¼ teaspoon dry mustard
- ¼ teaspoon *each* nutmeg and cayenne
- 1 cup ricotta cheese
- ¾ cup *each* grated Parmesan and Swiss cheese

1. Melt butter in medium-size skillet over medium-high heat. Add remaining filling ingredients and sauté until vegetables are tender and liquid is almost evaporated. Set aside.

2. Preheat oven to 425°F.

3. With an electric mixer, beat egg whites on high speed until they hold a stiff peak.

4. In separate bowl, beat egg yolks well; add remaining ingredients (except egg whites) and combine thoroughly.

5. Stir ⅓ of the whites into the yolk mixture. Fold in remaining whites.

6. Fill each of four 1-cup soufflé dishes half full of soufflé mixture, add ¼ of the mushroom filling, and top with remainder of soufflé mixture. Bake until puffed and golden (15 to 20 minutes). Serve immediately.

Because these soufflés are individual, they bake quickly in the oven and, with their delicious fillings, make an elegant meal at any time of the day.

Lemon-Butter Asparagus

- 1½ to 2 pounds asparagus Boiling salted water
- 2 tablespoons melted butter
- 1 tablespoon lemon juice Lemon wheels, for garnish

1. Wash asparagus and cut or snap off tough ends.

2. In a wide frying pan in a little boiling water, lay spears parallel, no more than 3 layers deep. Cook, uncovered, over high heat until stems are just tender when pierced with a fork (6 to 8 minutes). Drain.

3. Mix butter and lemon juice. Pour over asparagus; garnish with lemon wheels.

Fresh Fruit Platter

Provide an assortment of washed whole fruits. Attractively arranged, the fruit platter makes a lovely, edible centerpiece.

Croissants

Warm half a dozen purchased croissants in oven during last few minutes while soufflé bakes, or serve at room temperature.

COOKING PLAN

1. Assemble all ingredients and cooking equipment.

2. Chop vegetables for soufflé filling; sauté.

3. Preheat oven to 425°F.

4. Separate eggs and grate cheese for soufflé. Beat whites and yolks.

5. Combine soufflé ingredients and fill soufflé dishes. Bake.

6. Wash asparagus and fruit. Pat fruit dry and arrange on platter.

7. Heat water for asparagus; cook.

8. Warm croissants.

9. Melt butter for asparagus; add lemon juice.

To serve: Place fruit platter on table. Drain asparagus and top with lemon butter. Serve soufflés and croissants.

This brunch alternative to Eggs Benedict is designed for warming-tray serving, making it perfect for entertaining large groups. The rich entrée was developed for an ocean resort hotel, where the summer brunches were the talk of the town.

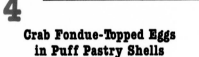

Crab Fondue-Topped Eggs in Puff Pastry Shells

Sliced Tomato and Avocado

Fresh Berry Basket

Wine suggestion:
Champagne

Crab Fondue-Topped Eggs in Puff Pastry Shells

Assemble the egg-filled shells yourself, or let each person put together his or her own. This is a fine menu for a buffet brunch because neither the eggs nor the fondue needs to be served immediately. Keep the fondue warm over very low heat.

- 2 tablespoons *each* butter and flour
- ¼ teaspoon *each* salt and cayenne
- 1¼ cups milk
- ¼ cup dry white wine *or* Champagne
- 4 tablespoons freshly grated Parmesan cheese
- 6 to 8 ounces thawed frozen *or* canned crabmeat, drained and flaked
- 4 baked puff pastry shells Heat-and-Hold Scrambled Eggs (recipe follows)
- 4 tablespoons minced fresh parsley

1. Melt butter in chafing dish or saucepan over medium-high heat. Tilt pan and stir in flour and seasonings. Blend well.

2. Add milk slowly, stirring briskly with a wooden spoon or wire whisk. Cook over medium heat, stirring constantly, until mixture boils and thickens.

3. Stir in wine, cheese, and crab; heat through.

4. Fill pastry shells with eggs. Spoon sauce over. Garnish with minced parsley.

Heat-and-Hold Scrambled Eggs

These eggs will not dry out, even if kept warm on an electric warming tray for as long as an hour.

- 2 teaspoons *each* butter and flour
- 3 tablespoons *each* plain yogurt and sour cream
- 8 to 10 eggs
- 1 tablespoon butter

1. In a small saucepan, melt the 2 teaspoons butter. Stir in flour and cook until bubbly. Remove from heat and blend in yogurt and sour cream. Return to heat and cook, stirring, until bubbly and smooth; set aside.

2. Beat eggs lightly. In a wide frying pan, melt the 1 tablespoon butter. Pour in eggs and allow to set. Run spatula around edge, lifting to allow uncooked eggs to flow underneath until eggs are softly set.

3. Remove from heat and gently stir in yogurt-sour cream mixture. Eggs can be served immediately or held, in a serving dish, on a warming tray.

Sliced Tomato and Avocado

Slice 2 large, fully ripe tomatoes and 1 avocado. Sprinkle avocado with lemon juice to keep it from darkening. Arrange on butter lettuce leaves. Provide cruets of vinegar and oil.

Fresh Berry Basket

Arrange whole, washed berries in a lined woven basket. Garnish with flowers. Serve with one of the flavored creams (recipes on page 84).

COOKING PLAN

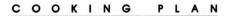

1. Assemble all ingredients and cooking equipment.

2. Bake pastry shells if frozen.

3. Grate cheese for fondue. Prepare and keep warm.

4. Cook eggs and keep warm.

5. Slice tomatoes and avocado. Wash and drain berries. Arrange in basket.

To serve: Place fruit, salad, and cruets on table. Assemble egg-filled shells and top with fondue, or let diners assemble their own.

Index